PSALMS 1–41

A Devotional Commentary

TONY BENNETT

DayOne

Scripture taken from the New International Version®. Copyright © 1978 by Hodder & Stoughton. Used by permission. All rights reserved.

Copyright © 2022 by Tony Bennett

First published in Great Britain in 2022

The right of Tony Bennett to be identified as the Author of this Work has been asserted by him in accordance with the Copyright, Designs and Patents Act 1988.

British Library Cataloguing in Publication Data
A record for this book is available from the British Library

ISBN: 978-1-84625-718-6

Cover design by Kathryn Chedgzoy

Printed by 4edge

DayOne, Ryelands Road, Leominster, HR6 8NZ
Email: sales@dayone.co.uk
Website: www.DayOne.co.uk

To Richard and Vicky Nicholl

'I do not cease to give thanks for you,
remembering you in my prayers'
(Eph. 1:16)

'Tony Bennett hits the spot by providing clear and insightful answers to three basic questions: What is this Psalm about? How does it speak to me? How does it lead me to Jesus? Read this book as a daily devotional or as stimulus for preaching and you will be blessed.'

Colin S. Smith, Senior Pastor, The Orchard, Arlington Heights, Chicago, USA

'What I especially liked about this book is that it is written by someone who is not just well informed about the Psalms, but who clearly uses the Psalms and is blessed by them. Tony Bennett is attentive to the Psalms in their original contexts, helps us see the fulness of their meaning in Christ, and then shows us how we can join in too. Reading these devotions is like having a friend alongside you, who not only points out things of interest, but who gently keeps asking, 'Is this a song you could sing as well?' I expect it to be a blessing to many.'

Revd Christopher Henderson, Pastor, Anchor Church, Lymington & Pennington, Hampshire, UK

CONTENTS

FOREWORD

Humbled, comforted, challenged, engaged—these were my emotions as I read this profoundly timely book on Psalms 1–41.

Firstly humbled: I found myself humbled, because of the personal context, in which Tony Bennett wrote this book. These were his comments on Psalm 11:5, '"The LORD examines the righteous." As I write this, my dear wife Sue has been undergoing treatment for two years for cancer. Physically she is quite weak, but spiritually she is still allowing God to test and refine her, as he prepares her for her call to glory.' I had the privilege of preaching at Tony's marriage to Sue at Christ Church, Clifton, on 9 December 2006 and you should have heard the sustained cheering as they were pronounced 'Husband and Wife'. It went on and on. I'd honestly never heard anything like it at a wedding and it spoke of how Sue was just adored by so many. She had real charisma and eyes that danced with her confidence and joy in the Lord. So it's humbling to read a commentary calling us all to trust God, that was written amid the shadow of the loss of the love of one's life.

Second comforted: I've always paid attention to Psalm 16, ever since Richard Bewes, a former Rector of All Souls Church, told me that verse 11 was Billy Graham's favourite verse in the Bible. But on this occasion, I found Tony brought verses 1 to 4 alive to me, as he asks, whilst expounding verse 1, '"Preserve me O God, for in you I take refuge." What do children do when they awake afraid at night? They run to their parents' room, and in the same way David runs to God.' I have a six-year-old daughter called Mercy and she now reminds me of Psalm 16:1 constantly! And of course, how we have needed to hear these words of comfort that come again and again in these psalms, in a world that is reeling from the economic, environmental, emotional, mental, physical and spiritual impacts of Covid-19. Brothers and sisters, we all need to go deeper into God, and not just hear from our favourite psalms, but to find this theme of comfort consecutively, as we see the psalmist face trial after trial in psalm after psalm.

Third, challenged: as you may well know from Psalm 1, this doorway to the spiritual life of Israel, an underlying theme in Book I of the Psalms, is that of the righteous and the wicked, the different lives they live, the different way God views them and their final destiny. And this commentary kept reminding me that eternity was at stake in the choices I make. Tony's doctorate is in American Politics and in his life teaching that subject it's obvious he learnt to construct questions that made his students think through the key issues at stake in the subject being taught. He brings those same analytical skills to bear in his points of reflection at the end of each chapter. You'll find that his comments and questions have you chewing on the text for the rest of the day. And wonderfully they reflect a profoundly Christocentric handling of this part of the Old Testament.

Lastly, engaged: you may not know that Tony wrote a seminal text book for the study of American Politics. So, though he's very much an Englishman, he has a great love of the USA, and this means that the illustrations in the book are truly engaging. So we visit the Rio Grande with Psalm 1, NASA with Psalm 8, Harvard with Psalm 9, and so it goes on. And one has to say it's a relief that Agincourt gets a mention in Psalm 20! But the illustrations keep coming and they provide light and depth.

So that's what I felt as I read this incredibly helpful commentary on the first book of the Psalms: humbled, comforted, challenged and engaged! I'm sure you'll feel the same. We owe Tony a great debt for labouring as he has for all of our greater good.

Rico Tice
Senior Minister (Evangelism), All Souls Church, London

PREFACE

> A Christian community without the Psalter has
> lost an incomparable treasure, and by taking it
> back into use will recover resources it never
> dreamed it had.
>
> Dietrich Bonhoeffer, *The Psalms:*
> *Prayer Book of the Bible*, 1940

For as long as I can recall I have read a psalm each day as part of my morning devotions. In doing so, one reads through the 150 psalms every five months. In one sense, I therefore came to know the psalms very well and particular verses from favourite psalms were known by heart. But more recently I came to realise that if someone asked me the same question that Philip asked of the Ethiopian official in Acts 8:30—'Do you understand what you are reading?'—I might give the same answer, 'How can I, unless someone guides me?' (Acts 8:31).

This project was born on the morning of 29 June 2019. I had just completed the manuscript for my third devotional book for Day One. The short, 1300-word expositions had become something of a trademark, and I wondered about bringing the same format to the psalms. And I needed a project—something to fill my time and to warm my heart as days became ever more testing. My dear wife Sue was into her second year of chemotherapy treatment for secondary breast cancer. We were, therefore, inevitably very much 'at home' and I felt I needed something to profitably fill the hours that were not taken up with caring for her. What a blessing it turned out to be! Progress was slow to start with but then came the first Covid lockdown and we were now not only 'at home' but 'home alone'! So, by the end of the summer 2020 I had completed Book I of the Psalter.

The Psalter is made up of five books of unequal length. Book I (Ps. 1–41) is made up almost exclusively of psalms of David. There are themes to watch out for too: the paths and destinations of the righteous and the wicked; the potential evil of the tongue; the life of holiness; waiting on God; the frailty of human life. Many of the psalms focus on the character and attributes of God—who God is and what he is like—and it's important to know God if we want to worship and praise him aright. As someone put it, 'You need a *theology* before you can have a *doxology*!' But these attributes of God need to be understood and applied personally. For David, the Lord isn't just '*a* shepherd' or even '*the* shepherd', he is '*my* shepherd' (Ps. 23:1). He is also my portion (16:5), my strength (18:1), my rock, my fortress, my deliverer, my God, my refuge, my shield, the horn of my salvation and my stronghold (18:2), my light and my salvation (27:1)!

Reading through the psalms consecutively allows us to pick up these themes more clearly and to experience the wonderful range of human emotions that they depict—psalms of worship and praise, psalms of sorrow and despair, psalms (as it were) in both the major and the minor key. And we see within them the unvarnished honesty of the psalmist that finds no wish or need to attempt to conceal his true emotions from the God who already knows the very secrets of our hearts.

For each psalm, I aim to show its historical setting, explain its meaning, apply its teaching to our daily lives, and see how the psalmist points us to the Lord Jesus Christ. My prayer is that these short devotional expositions will be as great a blessing to my readers as they were to me in their writing. May you be able to join with the psalmist in saying:

> The LORD is my strength and my shield;
> in him my heart trusts, and I am helped;
> my heart exults,
> and with my song I give thanks to him. (Ps. 28:7)

Tony Bennett
Lymington, Hampshire
January 2022

PSALM 1

When we walk with the Lord

Some years ago, I was driving to the small town of Red River in the mountains of northern New Mexico. Having passed through Santa Fe and Taos, I should have forked right to Arroyo Hondo but I decided to stay on Route 64 in order to cross the Rio Grande Gorge Bridge with its spectacular view of the river 600 feet below. Having stopped for the obligatory photographs I pressed on, having seen there was a road off to the right taking me back across the Rio Grande and back to the road I should have taken. I turned right but the road quickly became a rocky track before descending in a series of frightening hairpin bends to the valley floor. There in front of me were the waters of the Rio Grande—but no bridge. It had been swept away in floods the previous winter. The moral is that the road you take determines your destination.

The Bible often speaks of our life as being a choice between two paths which have two very different destinies. In Genesis 13, we read of Lot making a choice between two paths: 'And Lot lifted up his eyes and saw that the Jordan Valley was well watered everywhere like the garden of the LORD, like the land of Egypt' (Gen. 13:10). And that's the route Lot chose—'and he moved his tent

13

as far as Sodom' (13:12). The consequences were utterly disastrous, and for his wife they were deadly. Then at the beginning of the New Testament, Jesus speaks of two gates and two roads: 'Enter by the narrow gate. For the gate is wide and the way is easy that leads to destruction, and those who enter by it are many. For the gate is narrow and the way hard that leads to life, and those who find it are few' (Matt. 7:13–14).

Between these two comes Psalm 1 that talks about 'the way of the righteous' and 'the way of the wicked' (v. 6)—what one commentator calls 'the way of life' and 'the way of doom.'[1] And the fact that this is the focus of the first psalm is saying to us that nothing matters more than choosing the right path if we want to get safely to the right destination. It's the biblical doctrine of the two ways—and there is, says God, no 'third way.' Although the psalm depicts these two ways, the way of the righteous is given three verses (vv. 1–3), the way of the wicked just one (v. 4), with two concluding and comparative verses (vv. 5–6). Let's look at the psalm in those three parts.

The first thing we're told of the righteous is that they are 'blessed'. The word has the meaning of 'happy', 'fulfilled.' In the Hebrew, it's a plural word, so literally 'O the blessednesses of the man[2] ...' But having established what the righteous person is, the psalmist immediately tells us three things that he does *not* do. In other words, the psalmist starts where each of us starts—as sinners.

14

This blessed, righteous person 'walks not in the counsel of the wicked, nor stands in the way of sinners, nor sits in the seat of scoffers' (v. 1). What these lines depict is the downward spiral into sin. You can see it in the choices that Lot made: he parts company with Abraham (Gen. 13:11); then he pitches his tent toward Sodom (13:12); he moves into the city (14:12); finally, we find him sitting in the gateway with the city's elders (19:1). How easy it is to slip into the way of the wicked. The first steps seem so innocuous. That's why resisting temptation right at the start is so important—what Dale Ralph Davis describes as 'the vacuum-cleaner power-moves' that sin puts on us.[3]

Then we're told the positive sign of the righteous person: 'His delight is in the law of the LORD, and on his law he meditates day and night' (v. 2). The 'law of the LORD' refers to Scripture as a whole. And notice that he doesn't just read it, he's totally pre-occupied with it—day and night—and he meditates on it. So why are you reading the Bible? Why are you reading the Psalms? There are two good inter-related reasons: because they show us clearly the way of salvation; because they show us Christ—yes, even the Old Testament. Jesus told the crowds that the Scriptures 'bear witness about me' (Jn. 5:39), and he told the Sadducees that they were wrong in their religious beliefs 'because you know neither the Scriptures nor the power of God' (Matt. 22:29). Is reading and hearing the Scriptures preached a drudgery, for you? Is it a chore? Is it just a habit? Or can you truly say with the psalmist that God's Word 'is better to me than thousands of gold and silver pieces' (Ps. 119:72)?

Psalm 1 contains two pictures— one of the righteous person and one of the wicked.

Psalm 1 contains two pictures— one of the righteous person and one of the wicked. The righteous, says the psalmist, 'is like a tree planted by streams of water' (v. 3). What's more, this is a fruitful tree and it's an evergreen—'its leaf does not wither.' Dale Ralph Davis teaches verse 3 by telling us that this tree has stability (it's planted), vitality (it's by streams of water), productivity (it yields fruit), durability (it does not wither) and prosperity![4] The tree planted by water is an oft-used biblical metaphor. And this is a wonderful picture of the true Christian who is living close to Christ. And Jesus himself echoes the same truths when he preaches to the crowds: 'If anyone thirsts, let him come to me and drink' (Jn. 7:37), and it's the same 'living water' of which Jesus spoke to the woman of Samaria at the well (Jn. 4:13–14). What is more, the apostle Paul tells us about the fruit of the righteous person: 'love, joy, peace, patience, kindness, goodness, faithfulness, gentleness, self-control' (Gal. 5:22–23).

Then comes the stark contrast—'Not so the wicked' being the literal translation of the opening of verse 4. And there's a picture for them too, for they are 'like chaff'—fruitless and worthless, blown away by the wind of God's judgement (v. 5) to perish eternally (v. 6). The fruitful tree and the chaff are two dramatic pictures and should cause each one of us to pause and ask which one am I? Am I, by God's grace, the fruitful tree with my roots in the living water of God's Word, or am I the rootless chaff about to be blown away to eternal ruin?

One final thought. There has ever been only One truly 'blessed man' who never walked in the counsel of the wicked, nor stood in the way of sinners, nor sat in the seat of scoffers; only One who truly delighted in God's Word and meditated upon it day and night. And therefore the first verse of the first psalm points us to none other than the Lord Jesus Christ through whom the 'blessings' of verse 1 become ours as we trust in his death and resurrection and thereby have his righteousness imputed to our account, or as the apostle Paul tells us of Christ: 'For our sake [God] made him to be sin who knew no sin, so that in him we might become the righteousness of God' (2 Cor. 5:21). In life we often ask, 'Which way?' God asks us the same question. And Jesus tells us, 'I am the way, and the truth, and the life. No one comes to the Father except through

In life we often ask, 'Which way?' God asks us the same question.

me' (Jn. 14:6). Have you come to your senses, turned around and found the right path? For 'the way is hard that leads to life, and those who find it are few.' Which way are you walking?

REFLECT ON THESE POINTS:

- The road you take determines your destination.
- How easy it is to slip into the way of the wicked. The first steps seem so innocuous.
- Can you truly say with the psalmist that God's Word 'is better to me than thousands of gold and silver pieces' (Ps. 119:72)?

PSALM 2

Rejoice! The Lord is King

Around Easter 2014, British prime minister David Cameron stated that in his opinion Britain was 'a Christian country' and urged Christians to 'be more evangelical about their faith.'[1] His statement was, in itself, unremarkable, but the reaction was predictable. Within a few days, an open letter signed by 56 eminent intellectuals was published in *The Daily Telegraph* accusing the prime minister of fanning the flames of sectarian division. Now I'm sure there were many valid reactions to Mr. Cameron's remarks from 'well said' to wondering whether his 'doing God' had anything to do with a not so far off general election, but why did such bland remarks cause such outrage amongst such highly educated people? What is it about Jesus Christ that engenders such rage? And that's exactly what David asks at the start of Psalm 2—'Why?' 'Why do people rage and plot against God's Anointed—the LORD Jesus Christ?' This is a psalm in which we hear four voices: of the psalmist-narrator; of the rebellious nations; of God the Father; and of God the Son. Let us consider each voice in turn.

The psalm begins (vv. 1–2) with the psalmist-narrator—whom Luke identifies as David (Acts 4:25)—asking why 'the nations', 'the peoples' and their 'kings' are raging and plotting against God's Anointed One. This insurrection is not limited to any country or continent, nor to any class of people. This is worldwide, universal rebellion. It happens on the London Underground and at 35,000 feet over the Pacific, in the Brazilian rainforests and in the Arctic tundra. And it's happened throughout history: in David's time, in Jesus' time and in our own time.

Then in verse 3, we hear the voice of the rebellious nations. And what they're saying is very similar to the words of the rebellious citizens in Jesus' parable: 'We do not want this man to reign over us' (Lk. 19:14). And nowhere is this rebellion seen more clearly than in the events leading up to the death of the Lord Jesus Christ. For the New Testament records how people 'plotted' and 'took counsel' against Jesus. Mark records early in his gospel that the Pharisees 'plotted with the Herodians against [Jesus], how they might destroy him' (3:6, NKJV). And Matthew records how 'all the chief priests and elders of the people took counsel against Jesus to put him to death' (27:1). As the eminent preacher Charles Spurgeon wrote: 'We have in these verses a description of the hatred of human nature against the Christ of God.'[2] Indeed, this is what sin is—the

This is what sin is—the repudiation of God's rule in favour of one's own will.

repudiation of God's rule in favour of one's own will. And what we see in verses 1–2 is, as one commentator puts it, 'that in the heart of every person there is a basic rebellion against God such that faced God's own Son and his claim to be our rightful Lord and King.'[3]

And why do they rebel? Because they falsely accuse God of trying to enslave them, and hence they want to 'burst their bonds apart and cast away their cords' (v. 3). Our rebellion is a quest for freedom from authority. When God's will clashes with our will, we utter these same sentiments giving voice to our belief that God is a harsh ruler who wants to enslave us. But the sad and ironic thing is that these 'cords' we want to cast off are cords of a Father's love. As God says to his people through the prophet Hosea: 'I led them with cords of kindness, with the bands of love' (11:4). It is Jesus who tells us that 'my yoke is easy, and my burden is light' (Matt. 11:30).

Next, we read of God's response to this angry plotting—first as reported by the psalmist (vv. 4–5) and second directly from the mouth of God the Father (v. 6). God's response, we read, is twofold: derisory laughter (v. 4) and wrathful fury (v. 5). This is one of only a few places in Scripture where God is said to laugh—not because he takes sin lightly, but because those who rage at him are fools and derision is, therefore, the appropriate response. Indeed, God's mocking laughter is 'part of his judgement on unrepentant sinners.'[4] God's laughter and derision may be somewhat disconcerting, but as Michael Wilcock comments: 'it is what God says that should really worry us' for, as the psalmist tells us God will 'speak to them in his wrath and terrify them in his fury' (v. 5). One wonders what the aforementioned 56 intellectuals would have said had David Cameron mentioned that! You see, after all the hectoring and harrumphing of God's enemies, God follows their 'Let us . . .' with his 'As for me . . .' as he has already decided what he will do: 'I have set my King on Zion, my holy hill' (v. 6). And if they realised the significance of those words, they would indeed strike terror into every God-scorning intellectual, chat show host, business tycoon, politician—and, yes, into you and me if we have as yet failed to bow the knee to God's King and acknowledge his worldwide and eternal authority.

The fourth voice we hear is that of God's King—the Lord Jesus Christ. For here we have words that are echoed by God both at Jesus' baptism (Matt. 3:17) and his transfiguration (Matt. 17:5)—'You are my Son' (v. 7)—and the apostle Paul uses them in reference to Jesus' resurrection (Acts 13:33). Who cannot be unmoved by the fate that will befall those who persist to the end in their opposition to God's Son— to be 'dashed in pieces like a potter's vessel' (v. 9)? Here is imagery frequently used by Isaiah and Jeremiah to illustrate the awful consequences of God's righteous anger at our sin. As the writer to the Hebrews reminds us: 'It is a fearful thing to fall into the hands of the living God' (Heb. 10:31).

It is against that dreadful warning that David ends the psalm with words of advice: we are to 'be wise' and 'be warned' (v. 10), to 'serve him with fear' and 'rejoice with trembling' (v. 11). Is this your response to God's one and only Son? So how are we to obey these instructions?

Do you want spiritual wisdom? Scripture tells us that 'the fear of the LORD is the beginning of wisdom' (Prov. 9:10). Do you want to hear God's warnings? The apostle Paul tells us that 'All Scripture is breathed **Do you want to hear God's warnings?** out by God and profitable for teaching, for reproof, for correction, and for training in righteousness' (2 Tim. 3:16). Finally, in verse 12, we have the psalmist's final instruction: 'Kiss the Son, lest he be angry, and you perish in the way.' The kiss is a kiss of homage so what we have here is a command to pay homage to the Lord Jesus Christ. And there's an unmistakable incentive in the form of a reminder that the only refuge from the wrath of God is to be found in the sacrifice of Jesus on Calvary. Failure to offer that homage will lead to our perishing—to eternal death and separation from God. But the psalm closes with an echo of the opening of Psalm 1. There we were told that 'Blessed is the man' who walks in God's path. Here we are assured that 'Blessed are all who take refuge in him'—that is, in Christ. So, rejoice, the Lord is King! But is he your king?

> He sits at God's right hand,
> Till all His foes submit,
> And bow to His command,
> And fall beneath His feet.
> Lift up your heart, lift up your voice,
> Rejoice, again I say, rejoice.[5]

REFLECT ON THESE POINTS:

- 'We have in these verses a description of the hatred of human nature against the Christ of God.' (Charles Spurgeon)
- The sad and ironic thing is that these 'cords' we want to cast off are cords of a Father's love.
- The only refuge from the wrath of God is to be found in the sacrifice of Jesus on Calvary.

PSALM 3

Salvation belongs to our God

This is the first psalm to include a superscription giving the historical context of its writing—'A Psalm of David, when he fled from Absalom his son' which puts the biblical context as 2 Samuel 15–16. King David had been overly-occupied with the affairs of state, allowing an opening for his son Absalom to 'steal the hearts of the men of Israel' (2 Sam. 15:6). Absalom's subsequent rebellion was so sudden that David fled from Jerusalem and it was whilst David was fleeing that he was insulted and cursed by Shimei (2 Sam. 16:5–14), a relative of his predecessor King Saul. That is the context, we are told, of David writing this psalm. The psalm falls into four two-verse stanzas.

In the first two psalms, life for the godly person seemed to be nothing but 'blessed' (1:1; 2:12). Having read them, the struggling Christian might think: 'Well, that's all well and good in theory, but it's not what I experience in my daily life.' The trouble is that we, like David the author of this psalm, live in what has been called 'the gap between promise and reality'—we experience the difference between what God has promised and what we see now.[1]

In verses 1–2, we hear of the troubles we face.[2] And

trouble is common to all—even to Jesus. David's foes are 'many'—the word appears three times—and their numbers are growing. Indeed, the opening line is better rendered: 'How have they *increased* that trouble me' (v. 1, NKJV). And how often do we feel that our troubles are multiplying, almost overwhelming us? And so we learn that though 'blessed' by God, the godly are not immune from suffering and pain. But where do they turn?

In verses 3–4, we hear of the God whom we trust. The focus changes with the opening words of verse 3: 'But you, O LORD . . .' And in his multiplying troubles, David turns to contemplate the attributes of his God—his shield, his glory, the lifter up of his head (v. 3), and the God who answers prayer (v. 4). As one noted Bible preacher states: 'A spiritual and saving knowledge of God is the greatest need of every human creature. An unknown God can neither be trusted, served, nor worshiped.'[3] And David recites four attributes of God. First, 'you are a shield about me,' says David. Twenty-six times in the Old Testament God is described as a shield, and twelve of those descriptions are by David. Given the context, the military language is appropriate. A vast army is pursuing David, so what hope does he have? But David's divine shield is better than a military one for this shield is

> **'An unknown God can neither be trusted, served, nor worshiped.'**

'about' David—literally covers him, protecting him on all sides.

Secondly, David tells us that God is 'my glory,' literally 'my Glorious One.' David's own glory may be under attack, but God's glory is untouchable and unimpeachable.

And thirdly, for David, God is 'the lifter of my head.' Echoes here of Pharaoh's imprisoned cupbearer's dream and Joseph's interpretation that 'in three days Pharaoh will *lift up your head* and restore you to your office' (Gen. 40:13). Thus God promises to restore David's dignity and honour—recorded in 2 Samuel 19.

But not only does David remind himself that our God is a protecting God, a sufficient God and a restoring God, but also that he is an accessible God.[4] 'I cried aloud,' says David, 'and [God] answered'—or literally, 'keeps on answering.' In saying this, David is clearly looking back to previous times in his life when this has been true. And how good it is in the midst of trouble to look back and remember God's past faithfulness for it enables us more readily to trust him for today and for the future. As one hymn writer puts it:

> We'll praise Him for all that is past,
> We'll trust Him for all that's to come.[5]

In the third stanza, we read of the peace we enjoy. But it's important to notice that this is not peace because God has delivered us *from* our troubles, but peace *in the midst*

27

of those troubles. The 'many foes' of verse 3 are still there. Indeed, by verse 6 they are the 'many thousands'! But reading these truths in the Christian era, we hear the echo of our Lord saying to us: 'Peace I leave with you; my peace I give to you. Not as the world gives do I give to you. Let not your hearts be troubled, neither let them be afraid' (Jn. 14:27); 'In the world you will have tribulation. But take heart; I have overcome the world' (Jn. 16:33).

Which takes us to the psalm's final stanza in which we read of the salvation we receive. Salvation speaks of deliverance, and for David in his immediate situation, deliverance from his enemies. And this is where verse 7 fits in with its prayer that God may 'strike all my enemies on the cheek' and 'break the teeth of the wicked.' Such imprecations appear throughout the Psalter and many churches, unwilling to accept the concept of a wrathful God, either miss out those psalms altogether or just omit the 'offending' verses. So Psalm 95 will be cut after verse 7, or Psalm 137 after verse 6. But to anyone who takes God and the Bible seriously, that is clearly unacceptable.

There are two things we need to see in verse 7. First, that it is God and not us who does the avenging. Second, that it is not a God who is wrathful against sin and those who perpetrate it that is a moral outrage, but rather it is it *would* be an outrage if God was *not* wrathful against sin and those who practise it. Third, David's deliverance will come about only through the downfall of his enemies.

But whereas we like to pray prayers that are bland and sanitised, the Bible is more realistic. As Alec Motyer puts it: 'Where we leave implications unsaid, the Bible puts them into words; where we shelter behind innocuous requests, the Bible makes their implications also part of the way it prays. But prayer leaves the outcome in the hands of the Lord, the only place where it can be left with safety.'[6]

Whereas we like to pray prayers that are bland and sanitised, the Bible is more realistic.

But for us, salvation speaks of deliverance from the slavery and consequences of sin. And what a great truth David announces in the final verse: 'Salvation belongs to the LORD.' He alone has the power to save. And this Old Testament truth finds its true fulfilment not in David's victory over Absalom, but in the incarnation, life, death, resurrection and ascension of the Lord Jesus Christ—the One so named by God the Father 'for he shall save his people from their sins' (Matt. 1:21) and thereby God's blessing [will] be on God's people! As a contemporary hymn writer puts it:

> Salvation belongs to our God,
> Who sits on the throne and unto the Lamb.
> Praise and glory, wisdom and thanks,
> Honour and power and strength,
> Be to our God forever and ever, Amen.[7]

In the troubles you face, is this the God whom you trust? Is this the peace you enjoy? Is this the salvation you have received—only through the gracious work of the Lord Jesus Christ? If he is, and if it is then you can say with David:

> I lay down and slept;
> I woke again, for the LORD sustained me (v. 5).

Thanks be to God!

REFLECT ON THESE POINTS:

- 'A spiritual and saving knowledge of God is the greatest need of every human creature. An unknown God can neither be trusted, served, nor worshiped.' (A.W. Pink)
- How good it is in the midst of trouble to look back and remember God's past faithfulness for it enables us more readily to trust him for today and for the future.

PSALM 4

Round me falls the night

On the evening of 28 October 1980, television sets in 60 million American homes were tuned to watch the one-off debate between Jimmy Carter, who had just served as president for four years, and Governor Ronald Reagan. Election day was just five days away. As the debate was about to conclude, each candidate was given time to make a closing statement. Carter went first and told how he had talked about nuclear weapons with his 13-year-old daughter Amy. Then it was Reagan's time. Looking straight into the camera he began:

> Next Tuesday, all of you will go to the polls and make a decision. I think when you make that decision, it might be well if you would ask yourself, are you better off than you were four years ago?[1]

We don't know for sure what the exact context is for Psalm 4, but there's a hint that, rather like America under President Carter, the economy wasn't fairing too well, especially on the farm. And the psalm, as it were, poses a question: 'Can I still trust God even when life is not going well?' It's a question no doubt each of us has asked.

There are a number of common themes between this

psalm and its predecessor. In both, David is concerned about 'the many' who are troubling him—Psalm 3:1–2 and Psalm 4:6. In both, David talks of the God who hears and answers prayer—3:4 and 4:1, 3. And in both, David talks of seeking rest in sleep which is why Psalm 3 has been called a morning psalm—'I lay down and slept; I woke again (v. 5)—and Psalm 4 an evening psalm with its closing words: 'In peace I will both lie down and sleep' (v. 8). Like Psalm 3, this psalm features the God I can trust.

David begins with a plea to God to answer him and, as in Psalm 3, he strengthens himself by remembering God's attributes. You need to know God before you can trust him. In pleading for God to answer him, David calls to the 'God of my righteousness,' or literally 'my righteous God,' the One who always does what is right. To know and believe that truth alone brings great solace to the troubled believer. And it's what the apostle Paul assures us in the New Testament that 'for those who love God all things work together for good' (Rom. 8:28)—but notice to whom that promise is made.

You need to know God before you can trust him.

Having first addressed God, David then turns to those who are troubling him (vv. 2–5). First, in verse 2, he rebukes them for dishonouring him, even though he is king and therefore God's anointed one. How easy it is in these days to join with everyone else in denigrating our leaders. But

Scripture urges us that we pray 'for kings and all who are in high positions, that we may lead a peaceful and quiet life' (1 Tim. 2:2). Second, in verse 3, in what appears to be an aside to himself, David remembers that God will not abandon those whom he has 'set apart for himself.' And Scripture again backs him up as the apostle Paul writes of his confidence 'that he who began a good work in you will bring it to completion at the day of Jesus Christ' (Phil. 1:6).

> **God will not abandon those whom he has 'set apart for himself.'**

And third, returning to his adversaries, David tells them that they need to repent (vv. 4–5). The phrase 'be angry' (v. 4) means literally 'tremble', or as the King James Version has it, 'stand in awe.' It is only when we see God in all his awesome holiness and tremble before him, that we will have a right view of the awfulness of our sin. Only when we see God aright and turn away from 'the way of the wicked' (Ps. 1:6) will we be able to 'offer right sacrifices' (v. 5)—that is true worship—and 'trust in the LORD.'

Thus far, David has made a plea to God and addressed his oppressors. Finally, David preaches to himself through Scripture (vv. 6–8). It's a highly recommended recipe. But to do so, you need to know your Bible—and your God. In verse 6, we eavesdrop on David talking with himself: 'There are many who say, "Who will show us some good?"' David is quoting the conversation of the godless, or of those who choose their 'gods' according as to which one gives them the best 'stuff'. To take liberties with Ronald Reagan: 'Under which "god" will I be better off than I was four years ago?' they muse. But as James Johnston rightly and starkly reminds us: 'God doesn't just give us stuff—he gives us himself!'[2] And so David's response to the utilitarian question asked in the first half of verse 6 is for him to pray in Scripture as he paraphrases Aaron's blessing from Numbers 6:24–26:

> The LORD bless you and keep you;
> the LORD make his face to shine upon you and
>   be gracious to you;
> the LORD lift up his countenance upon you and
>   give you peace.

Suddenly, David realises that he's far better off with God than with mere earthly stuff—even with grain and wine in abundance. Have you come to that realisation? Are you truly satisfied with God alone, or is your heart still set on the temporal and passing things of this fleeting world? Can you sing from your heart these words made famous by George Beverly Shea?

> I'd rather have Jesus than silver or gold,
> I'd rather be His than have riches untold;
> I'd rather have Jesus than houses or lands,
> I'd rather be led by His nail-pierced hand;
> Than to be the king of a vast domain

And be held in sin's dread sway;
I'd rather have Jesus than anything
This world affords today.[3]

If you can, then you will also be able to echo David in the closing verse of this psalm:

In peace I will both lie down and sleep;
for you alone, O LORD, make me dwell in safety.

So if you're awake of a night, don't count sheep, recite psalms—and remember with grateful thanks the holy, merciful and faithful God of which they speak.

Round me falls the night;
Saviour, be my light:
Through the hours in darkness shrouded
Let me see Thy face unclouded;
Let Thy glory shine
In this heart of mine.[4]

REFLECT ON THESE POINTS:

- You need to know God before you can trust him.
- It is only when we see God in all his awesome holiness and tremble before him, that we will have a right view of the awfulness of our sin.
- David realises that he's far better off with God than with mere earthly stuff—even with grain and wine in abundance. Have you come to that realisation? Are you truly satisfied with God alone?

PSALM 5

Just as I am

A woman was going to a photographer's studio to have her picture taken. Beforehand, she visited her local beauty parlour who, to put it delicately, had done their best for her. But the woman still took a lady friend along for moral support. She took her seat in the studio and fixed her pose for the camera. But while the photographer was adjusting the lights she said to him, 'Now be sure you do me justice.' The friend who'd accompanied her said with a twinkle, 'My dear, what you want is not justice but mercy!'

As we read through the psalms we find themes that recur. We've already seen one: the world being divided, in God's eyes, into two groups—the righteous and the wicked. Indeed, that theme appears again in this psalm. But another theme—which makes its first appearance in Psalm 5—is the mercy of God. Mercy is when God does *not* give us what we deserve, as distinct from grace which is when God *does* give us what we *don't* deserve. Both doctrinally and poetically, God's mercy is right at the centre of Psalm 5.

The structure of the psalm is of five stanzas, all addressed by David to God but in them the relationships alternate. In verses 1–3, 7–8 and 11–12, David is talking to God about the righteous; in verses 4–6 and 9–10, David is talking to God about the wicked. So the psalm has an ABABA construction, not unlike a rondo in music. And we're meant to notice the contrasts. So whereas the righteous pray (v. 2), worship (v. 7) and rejoice (v. 11); the wicked lie (v. 6), flatter (v. 9) and rebel (v. 10). What's more, God reacts differently to these two groups. David tells us that God hears (v. 3), leads (v. 8), protects (v. 11) and blesses (v. 12) the righteous; but he hates (v. 5), destroys (v. 6), abhors (v. 6) and casts out (v. 10) the wicked. So even from that brief sketch of this psalm, it's fairly obvious that which group you're in is a matter of the utmost importance. It literally is a matter of eternal life or death. We'll return to God's mercy shortly.

But this is also a psalm about prayer. First, we learn of the different ways we can pray. In verse 1, David is merely 'groaning'. The Hebrew word has connotations of one's innermost thoughts or sighings that are not able to be articulated. Do you feel so distraught at times that you can't even put your prayer into words? David felt like that. Indeed, he would write in another psalm: 'Even before a word is on my tongue, behold, O LORD, you know it altogether' (Ps. 139:4). By verse 2, his prayer is a 'cry'—literally 'the sound of my imploring.' Not until verse 3, does the psalmist seem to find his 'voice'. One commentator writes:

People who don't know God well think they have to pray with special words. Their prayers sound like a formula with set words and phrases. But if you know God, you can come to him without putting on your makeup. You pour out your unvarnished thoughts to him. If you had a good father, you talk to God the way you would talk to your dad—you are respectful but completely comfortable that he loves you and understands.[1]

Then in verses 4–8, we discover the basis upon which we can come to God in prayer. We can come to God in prayer because of the kind of God he is and what he has done for us. First, in verses 4–6, we find that our God is a holy God. No, the word 'holy' isn't actually there, but look at the six things these six lines tell us of him, that: he does not delight in wickedness (v. 4); evil may not dwell with him (v. 4); the boastful cannot stand before him (v. 5); he hates all evildoers (v. 5); he destroys the liars (v. 6); he 'abhors the bloodthirsty and deceitful man' (v. 6).

We can come to God in prayer because of the kind of God he is and what he has done for us.

So how do you respond to all that? You might be thinking: 'But I thought it was the case that "God hates the sin, but loves the sinner." Now I read that God "hates

38

all evildoers." How do I square that circle?' Two points. First, you won't find that axiom in Scripture. Second, it's a bit misleading. What one ought to say is, 'God hates the sin, but loves the *truly repentant* sinner.' And that's not the kind of person David is talking about in these verses. An 'evildoer' is someone who 'sins as a way of life.'[2] It is the unregenerate person whom the apostle Paul describes as being 'by nature children of wrath' (Eph. 2:3). And, says Paul, we all used to be like that. 'But God,' he continues, 'being rich in mercy'—there's that word again—'because of the great love with which he loved us, even when we were dead in our trespasses, made us alive together with Christ' (Eph. 2:4–5). So the question is: 'Can you say, with Paul, "But God, being rich in mercy . . . has made me alive together with Christ"?'

And that's exactly where David turns in verse 7 with his 'but . . .' Now David's just been reeling off the sins of these wicked people and so you might expect him to say something like: 'But I will enter your house . . . because I'm a much better person than them.' But no! That's not what David says, and I pray it's not what you're either saying or thinking right now. No! David is quite clear what is the only basis upon which he can come to this holy God— 'through the abundance of your steadfast love' (v. 7), or as the New King James Version has it: 'in the multitude of your mercy.' And there it is, right in the middle of the psalm—the most important place in Hebrew poetry that puts its climax in the middle, not at the end. As Dale Ralph Davis so succinctly puts it: 'David does not come on the basis of his religiosity... but only by grace.'[3]

> Just as I am—without one plea,
> But that Thy blood was shed for me,
> And that Thou bidst me come to Thee,
> O Lamb of God, I come.[4]

Is that how you come to God? It's the only way to come. And it's only because of God's mercy that we can pray with David: 'Lead me, O LORD, in your righteousness because of my enemies; make your way straight before me' (v. 8). It's only because of God's mercy that we can claim the psalm's final verse promise: 'For you bless the righteous, O LORD; you cover him with favour as with a shield' (v. 12). Because the only way we can be relieved of the debt of 'the abundance of [our] transgressions' (v. 10) is 'through the abundance of [God's] steadfast love'—the abundance of God's mercy (v. 7), and thereby we can say with the apostle Peter:

> Blessed be the God and Father of our Lord Jesus Christ, who according to His abundant mercy has begotten us again to a living hope through the resurrection of Jesus Christ from the dead, to an inheritance incorruptible and undefiled and that does not fade away, reserved in heaven for you.'
> (1 Peter 1:3–4, NKJV)

And so we can sing the final verse of the hymn I quoted above:

> Just as I am—of that free love
> The breadth, length, depth and height to prove,
> Here for a season, then above—
> O Lamb of God, I come.

REFLECT ON THESE POINTS:

- Mercy is when God does not give us what we deserve, as distinct from grace which is when God does give us what we don't deserve.
- David is quite clear what is the only basis upon which he can come to this holy God—'through the abundance of your steadfast love' (v. 7).

PSALM 6

No less days to sing God's praise

Aren't you just amazed at how honest and realistic the Bible is? And nowhere is this more evident than in the Psalms with its extraordinary—but very human—range of emotions. It's been said that much of the modern church seems to have forgotten how to sing in a minor key. Indeed, many of today's churches seem to have little room for penitential, soul-wrenching laments—like Psalm 6—which is also maybe why many churches have given up reading (or singing) their way through the Psalter as part of their corporate worship on the Lord's Day.

We are not told the exact context in which David penned this psalm. But traditionally, Psalm 6 has been categorised as a penitential psalm—along with Psalms 32, 38, 51, 102, 130 and 143—and used to be read on Ash Wednesday to begin a season of spiritual repentance during Lent. Others suggest that David is here facing trials brought on not by sin but by illness—hence 'heal me' and 'my bones are troubled' (v. 2), and the threat of death (v. 5). There are deep theological issues in this short psalm and so as to do justice to them, we'll focus on the first five verses.

In these verses, David makes a number of pleas to God. And it's important to notice what he is *not* asking from

God. Some translations render verse 1 as: 'Lord, do not rebuke me in your anger, or discipline me in your wrath' (NIV). But that's not really what David is asking. He's not asking God not to rebuke or discipline him. And neither should we. After all, Jesus tells us that 'those whom I *love*, I reprove and discipline' (Rev. 3:19). But what David asks is that God rebukes him, but not in his anger; that God disciplines him, but not in his wrath. And we can bring the same plea to God in times of trial and testing. It's how the prophet Jeremiah would pray some three centuries later: 'Correct me, O Lord, but in justice; not in your anger, lest you bring me to nothing' (Jer. 10:24). And David bases his plea on God's grace (v. 2) and God's 'steadfast love'—his mercy (v. 4), a theme we saw in Psalm 5. And so should we. As Charles Spurgeon comments on these verses: 'What a plea this is! How prevalent it is with God! If we turn to justice, what plea can we urge? But if we turn to mercy we may still cry, notwithstanding the greatness of our guilt, "Save me, for Thy mercies' sake."'[1]

But notice too that these verses are saturated with God himself. He invokes God's name: 'O Lord', five times in the first four verses! Every plea is to God—both the two negative pleas in verse 1, and the four positive pleas in verses 2–4: 'be gracious to me, O Lord'; 'heal me, O Lord'; 'how long, O Lord?'; 'turn, O Lord'. The best way to pray in such circumstances is to talk to God about himself, and in his own words. But in doing so, we don't have to sacrifice our honesty. And in verse 3, David seems to be halfway through a plea to God when he veers away with the heartfelt cry, 'how long?' It's a question God had asked—of Pharaoh (Ex. 10:3), of Moses (Num. 14:11) and of Samuel (1 Sam. 16:1). It's a question the prophet Elijah famously asked of the Israelites on Mount Carmel (1 Kgs. 18:21). And it's a question asked of God in ten psalms.[2] But asking that question in the Christian era, we can take the context out of the earthly present—'O LORD, how long must I suffer this?'—into the heavenly future, and a looking forward to Christ's triumphal return. This was what Samuel J. Stone had in mind when he wrote:

> Yet saints their watch are keeping,
> Their cry goes up, 'How long?'
> And soon the night of weeping
> Shall be the morn of song.[3]

God can reshape any evil we experience in order to bring about his good purposes.

But I want to offer a word of caution here, especially if you, like David, are going through a time of great trial.[4] Yes God is sovereign and for those who are truly his, God can reshape any evil we experience in order to bring about his good purposes (Rom. 8:28). But to pass off such heart-wrenching experiences merely as 'divine discipline' can dull you to a true awareness of just how wrong pain and suffering are—just how contrary they are to God's will and intention for this world that he created and saw that 'it was very good' (Gen. 1:31). For no matter how much God graciously turns such physical and mental trials to your spiritual good—and you should be praying that he will— these things remain evil and do not become 'good' just because God can turn them to your good.

Then in verse 5, David gives God his reason for the pleas he has made: 'For in death there is no remembrance of you; in Sheol who will give you praise?' Godly folk in the Old Testament believed in an afterlife. Jesus teaches that in the gospels.[5] But their understanding was sketchy compared with ours in the Christian era. But there are glimpses of resurrection or translation in the stories of Enoch, Abraham and Elijah, and of their understanding of the afterlife in Job 19:23–27, Psalm 16:10 and Daniel 12:2–3. As Gerald Wilson explains:

> Unlike the Christian view of heavenly existence after death, there is no chorus of the faithful eternally singing the praises of God around his heavenly throne. Sheol is, by contrast, mute and silent.[6]

Dale Ralph Davis explains David's conversation with God in verse 5 like this:

> If I die, if I succumb, if my enemies get me, if you do not deliver me, there will be one less to praise

45

you, for I won't be able to sing 'Praise to the Lord, the Almighty, the King of creation' among your people.[7]

That's why David plays what he must have thought was his trump card in verse 5: 'Well God, if you want me to continue to sing your praises, then you better rescue me from the state I'm in!' As Charles Spurgeon rightly remarks: 'Churchyards are silent places: the vaults of the sepulchre echo not with songs. Damp earth covers dumb mouths.'[8] But living post-Christ, we can sing with the faith and confidence of John Newton:

> Yes, when this heart and flesh shall fail,
> And mortal life shall cease,
> I shall possess within the veil
> A life of joy and peace.
>
> When we've been there ten thousand years,
> Bright shining as the sun,
> We've no less days to sing God's praise
> Than when we first began.[9]

As Jesus told Martha upon arriving at the tomb of her brother Lazarus: 'I am the resurrection and the life. Whoever believes in me, though he die, yet shall he live' (Jn. 11:25). Do *you* believe? If you do then the passing trials of this world—harsh and harrowing as they can be— are but transient, but what Christ offers is eternal.

REFLECT ON THESE POINTS:

- No matter how much God graciously turns physical and mental trials to your spiritual good—and you should be praying that he will—these things remain evil and do not become 'good' just because God can turn them to your good.

- The best way to pray in such circumstances is to talk to God about himself, and in his own words. But in doing so, we don't have to sacrifice our honesty.

PSALM 7

Take it to the Lord in prayer

In the autumn of 1969 British prime minister Harold Wilson was angered by what he saw as the false accusations made about him and his government by the Conservatives led by Ted Heath. Addressing the Labour Party Conference, Wilson delivered this memorable line as a riposte to Heath and the Conservatives: 'If they stop telling lies about us, we'll stop telling the truth about them!'[1]

So what to do with false accusations? That's the dilemma David was facing when he penned Psalm 7. That much we know from the title—'A Shiggaion of David, which he sang to the LORD concerning the words of Cush, a Benjaminite.' A shiggaion is probably a term for a particular musical genre. The Bible is silent as to who Cush was, but the fact that he was of the tribe of Benjamin—the same tribe as King Saul—suggests that the events of this psalm date from the time when David was fleeing from Saul, maybe around 1 Samuel 20.

A children's rhyme would have us believe that 'sticks and stones can break my bones, but words can never hurt me,' but we probably all know from bitter experience how untrue that is. There seem to be three possible responses to false accusations. First, strongly protest our innocence—but that leaves us open to the accusation that 'methinks he doth protest too much,' to slightly misquote Shakespeare.[2] Second, respond in kind—but that merely brings us down to the level of our false accuser. Third, to—in the words of the old hymn—'take it to the Lord in prayer.[3] And that's David's response in Psalm 7.

The psalm seems to divide into five uneven stanzas. First, in verses 1–2, we see that God is our refuge. We've already seen God so described in Psalms 2:12 and 5:11. The National Weather Service in the USA tells you that faced with a tornado threat in your home, 'go to your basement or safe room.' And faced with times of trial and danger, we need to do the same thing, and our 'safe place' is God. As David has already told us: 'You alone, O LORD, make me dwell in safety' (Ps. 4:8). But these opening verses are also a prayer as David asks God to save him and deliver him. He once told Saul that 'the LORD [has] delivered me from the paw of the lion' (1 Sam. 17:37) and now he believes God will deliver him from these lion-like adversaries.

Then in verses 3–5, David claims his innocence. Now this is not David being self-righteous. He's not claiming sinless perfection, but he's examining himself in this particular situation and is ready to accept responsibility if the charges are true. It's what Alec Motyer calls 'the blessedness of having a clear conscience.[4] And this is a million miles away from our frequent complaints of, 'I don't know why this is happening to me. I've never done anyone any harm!' Those kind of self-pitying thoughts are often simply an example of when a good conscience is merely the sign of a bad memory! And that's not what's going on here with David. It shows why as Christ's true disciples we should be seeking to live unimpeachable lives. And Jesus tells us to expect false accusations: 'Blessed are you when others revile you and persecute you and utter all kinds of evil against you falsely on my account. Rejoice and be glad, for your reward is great in heaven, for so they persecuted the prophets who were before you' (Matt. 5:11–12). And as the apostle Paul teaches us, in such circumstances 'when reviled, we bless ... when slandered, we entreat' (1 Cor. 4:11–12). As former First Lady Michelle Obama so aptly put it: 'When they go low, we go high!'[5]

Then in verses 6–11, we see God as judge as David tells us of his longing for right to prevail, for justice to be done. That's why we ought to be able to face such trials with a greater sense of peace. After all, Jesus tells us that 'in the world you *will* have tribulation. But take heart, I have overcome the world' (Jn. 16:33). But we're often left asking that question from the previous psalm—'O LORD, how long?' (Ps. 6:3). Or we're tempted to agree with the nineteenth-century American poet who wrote of:

> Truth forever on the scaffold,
> Wrong forever on the throne.

But that poet, James Russell Lowell (1819–91), then saw 'the scaffold' as the cross of Christ, going on to write:

> Yet that Scaffold sways the future,
> And behind the dim unknown
> Standeth God within the shadow,
> Keeping watch above His own.[6]

Why is God indignant? Because he is utterly righteous and we are utterly sinful.

And here again, as in Psalm 1, we see that stark binary choice presented by the Judge 'who tests the minds and hearts' (v. 9), by 'a God who feels indignation every day' (v. 11). And why is God indignant? Because he is utterly righteous (v. 9) and we are utterly sinful. The question each of us must ask, therefore, is: 'Am I to be found amongst "the wicked" or "the righteous"' (v. 9)? And the fourth stanza will tell how we know which we are.

For in verses 12–16, we find the portrait of the wicked, of the unsaved sinner. And who is he? Simply put, he is the 'man [who] does not repent' (v. 12), who 'conceives evil and is pregnant with mischief and gives birth to lies' (v. 14). Of course, you may think that you can control sin. But you never will. Sin will always end up controlling you. That's what verse 15 tells us. For, says David, the unrepentant sinner is like someone who thinks himself so clever that he digs a deep pit to catch a wild animal, but he covers it over so well that he ends up falling into it himself! He's trapped in his own trap—'hoist with his own petard' as we say. And in verse 16, sin is a boomerang—'his mischief returns upon his own head.' But these verses also tell us what God will do with such a person—he will whet his sword, make ready his bow and prepare fiery arrows to shoot at him (vv. 12–13). Picture language it may be, but it doesn't sound like the end you'd be looking forward to. So how to avoid it?

Only one way, and we find it in the final stanza—the final verse. Clearly as an unrepentant sinner I have no righteousness of my own. My only hope is to repent—a spiritual 180-degree turn—and by God's grace, through faith, be granted 'his righteousness' (v. 17). To have received this free gift of salvation will set our hearts to join with David's as he ends this psalm in praise and worship, knowing the wonder of being able to truly say: 'O LORD my God, in you do I take refuge.'

> Are we weak and heavy-laden,
> Burdened with a load of care?

Precious Saviour, *still our refuge*:
Take it to the Lord in prayer.
Do your friends despise, forsake you?
Take it to the Lord in prayer;
In His arms He'll take and shield you,
You will find a solace there.[7]

REFLECT ON THESE POINTS:

- Why is God indignant? Because he is utterly righteous and we are utterly sinful.
- You may think that you can control sin. But you never will. Sin will always end up controlling you.
- As an unrepentant sinner I have no righteousness of my own. My only hope is to repent and by God's grace, through faith, be granted 'his righteousness' (v. 17).

PSALM 8

Then sings my soul

All of the psalms are God-breathed so it would be difficult—and probably wrong—to say anything negative about any of them. But some of the 150 psalms are real stand outs and have become especially beloved by God's people over the centuries. And most would put Psalm 8 in that list. C.S. Lewis describes this psalm as 'a short, exquisite lyric,' whilst to Derek Kidner Psalm 8 'is an unsurpassed example of what a hymn should be, celebrating as it does the glory and grace of God, rehearsing what he has done, and relating us and our world to him.'[1]

The psalm begins—and ends—by celebrating the majesty of God's name: 'O LORD, our Lord, how majestic is your name in all the earth!' (vv. 1, 9). In Hebrew poetry this literary device (an *inclusio*) acts like a pair of bookends, or like a picture-frame—drawing attention to the subject matter in between. And although in English the name 'Lord' is repeated, the different case of the letters in the two words alerts us to the fact that in Hebrew these are two different names—*Yahweh* (or Jehovah) and *Adonai*— meaning God and ruler or king. Back in Exodus 3 when Moses enquired of God as to his name, we read that 'God said to Moses, "I Am Who I Am."' Moses knew that God's power and authority were attached to his name. This is God's personal name—*Yahweh*. And as Gerald Wilson notes: 'The "name" of God is an extension of God himself. Where God chooses to place his name—in the land, in the temple, on his people—there God is also.[2] And as Christians, when we read of how 'majestic' is God's name, we should turn to the apostle Paul talking about the Lord Jesus Christ: 'Therefore God has highly exalted him and bestowed on him the name that is above every name, so that at the name of Jesus every knee should bow' (Phil. 2:9–10).

And we know that we should read Psalm 8 from a Christological perspective because the gospels record Jesus applying it to himself. So when Jesus accepts the children's praise of 'Hosanna to the Son of David' he quotes Psalm 8:2, and in so doing he makes a clear claim of deity—as well as implicitly placing the chief priests in the category of 'the enemy and the avenger.'

Then in verses 3–4, David reflects on the contrast between the majesty of God's creation as against the insignificance of mankind. Maybe David is recalling his life as a shepherd and those nights out under the clear skies gazing into the heavens. If you've ever gazed into the night sky away from the light pollution of towns and cities, you will have a feeling for what David writes. But with just the naked eye, we can see but a small part of 'the moon and the stars, which you have set in place' (v. 3). In January 2006, NASA launched its New Horizons interplanetary probe to Pluto. Travelling at over 36,000 mph it made its closest approach to Jupiter in February 2007. But it didn't arrive near to Pluto until July 2015—9½ years after leaving Cape Canaveral, having travelled some 3.22 billion miles! As one commentator writes: 'How astonishing that the God of this vast universe, the God who made it and orders it, should think of us and care for us!'[3]

'How astonishing that the God of this vast universe, the God who made it and orders it, should think of us and care for us!'

And experience of the night sky is a rich biblical theme. There's Abram's star-gazing experience in Genesis 15, and Jacob's night time vision of the heavenly ladder in Genesis 28. But looking some thousand years forward from David, other shepherds were 'keeping watch over their flocks by night' on the same Bethlehem hills. And, as Bishop Perowne in his commentary on the Psalms points out:

> But a brighter glory than the glory of the stars
> shone round about them; and they knew better
> than David himself the meaning of the words:
> 'LORD, what is man that Thou art mindful of him?'

For to them it was said by the angel, 'Unto you is born this day, in the city of David, a Saviour, which is Christ the Lord.'[4]

But then with the opening of verse 5 the theme of the psalm pivots from man's utter insignificance to man being crowned by God with 'glory and honour.' Verse 1 spoke of God's glory and now in verse 5 we, being made in God's image, reflect God's glory in a way that other parts of the creation do not. We have been made, David reminds us, 'a little lower than the angels' (v. 5, NKJV). Thus we have in verses 5–8 an echo of the creation story in Genesis 1 when God said, 'Let us make man in our image, after our likeness. And let them have dominion over the fish of the sea and over the birds of the heavens and over the livestock and over all the earth and over every creeping thing that creeps on the earth' (Gen. 1:26). Indeed, the Hebrew word for God in Genesis 1:26 (*Elohim*) is the same word David uses for the 'heavenly beings' or 'angels' in Psalm 8:5.

And yet we know from bitter experience that's not quite how things are today. True, Adam and Eve had this kind of authority back in the Garden, but those days are long gone. Even our rule over the animal kingdom is at best superficial, as I find each time I try to take our water-hating golden Labrador outside on a wet day! Mankind is not in control of this world. Indeed, we often fail to even control ourselves. And so once again, it is left to the New Testament—and specifically Jesus—to fulfil the promise of the Old. And this is what the writer to the Hebrews explains in his second chapter (vv. 5–9) when he quotes verses 4–6 of Psalm 8. James Johnston helpfully explains:

> It's obvious that creation is not under our control as human beings the way God originally intended. But creation is under the control of one man. Christ has risen from the dead, and everything is under his feet. Everything on earth submits to his authority. Psalm 8 is looking forward to the day when God's people will be renewed and take their rightful rule over the world.[5]

This is what Isaiah is looking forward to when he writes:

> The wolf shall dwell with the lamb,
> and the leopard shall lie down with the young goat,
> and the calf and the lion and the fattened calf
>   together;
> and a little child shall lead them ... (Is. 11:6).

So the true fulfilment of this psalm is still to come. Only when Christ returns, the whole of creation is renewed, and the souls of all true believers are reunited with their resurrected bodies shall we truly sing: 'O LORD, our Lord, how majestic is your name in all the earth!' Is that your true hope and expectation? It can be, but only when the

Christ who alone truly fulfils this psalm is truly your Saviour and Redeemer.

> O Lord my God! when I in awesome wonder
> Consider all the works Thy hand has made,
> I see the stars, I hear the rolling thunder,
> Thy power throughout the universe displayed;
>
> *Then sings my soul, my Saviour God, to Thee,*
> *How great Thou art, how great Thou art!*[6]

REFLECT ON THESE POINTS:

- Psalm 8 'is an unsurpassed example of what a hymn should be, celebrating the glory and grace of God, rehearsing what he has done, and relating us and our world to him.' (Derek Kidner)
- David reflects on the contrast between the majesty of God's creation as against the insignificance of mankind.
- Mankind is not in control of this world. Indeed, we often fail to even control ourselves.

PSALM 9

Holy is the Lord

In 1905, the philosophy department at Harvard University decided to name their new building after the American philosopher Ralph Waldo Emerson (1803–82), a former student of the university. There was to be an inscription across the front of the building and the professors decided that this should read 'Man is the measure of all things'—a quotation from the atheistic Greek philosopher Protagoras (c. 490–420 BC) suggesting that there is no absolute truth, only truth as determined by man. But the President of Harvard, Charles William Eliot (1834–1926), was having none of it, and he quietly overruled the professors' choice. So when they returned from their summer vacation, the professors found the building complete, and cut in stone across the front were the words, 'What is man that Thou art mindful of him?' James Johnston includes this story in his commentary on Psalm 9 before adding:

> This conflict between President Eliot and the faculty captures the heart of our rebellion against God. The human heart says, 'It's all about me. There is no one above me.' And David calls on God

to humble us with his overwhelming power and glory. 'Put them in fear, O LORD! Let the nations know that they are but men' (Ps. 9:20).[1]

If one asked the average church-goer to describe a psalm, the word 'praise' would probably come within their description. And there are blocks of psalms—95 to 100, 145 to 150—that are psalms of praise. But Psalm 9 is the first which, at least in its opening, can be called a psalm of praise. Most commentators suggest that the psalm divides into two unequal halves—verses 1–12 in which David praises God, and verses 13–20 in which he prays to God.

The psalm opens (vv. 1–2) with a wonderful declaration of intent:

> *I will* give thanks to the LORD with my whole heart;
> *I will* recount all of your wonderful deeds.
> *I will* be glad and exult in you;
> *I will* sing praise to your name, O Most High.

There are at least three things we need to learn from these opening verses. First, David's thankful worship and praise is from the heart—indeed, 'with my whole heart.' Later in the Psalter (for example, in Psalm 50), we shall find God condemning his people for formalism and hypocrisy—religion that is all outward and not inward. As Jesus tells the woman of Samaria: 'The true worshippers will worship the Father in spirit and truth' (Jn. 4:23)

61

meaning that our worship must come from deep within us—from our spirit, our soul, our heart. Second, looking back in thankfulness for all God's 'wonderful deeds' is the best way to fuel our praise. Third, do we share the psalmist's intent? Are you as determined as David that you 'will' give thanks, be glad, exult and sing praises to our great and merciful God? And living in the Christian era gives us—as one modern Christian song puts it—'ten thousand reasons for my heart to find' to keep praising God.[2]

Looking back in thankfulness for all God's 'wonderful deeds' is the best way to fuel our praise.

But all this raises the question of why we should praise God. After all, we rather despise people who are so vain and insecure that they need people telling them—and everyone else—how wonderful they are. In one of their first meetings in 2017, members of President Trump's cabinet did exactly that! Indeed, Vice President Pence capped them all by saying it was 'the greatest privilege of my life to serve as vice president to a president that's bringing real strength back to our nation!'[3] But we don't praise God to boost his ego—as if puny mankind could do that. No! We praise and worship God because he is worthy of it and because glorifying God is 'the chief end of man.'[4] And David goes on to praise God for his deliverance (vv. 3–4), his justice (vv. 5–6), his eternal rule (vv. 7–8) and his protection of the oppressed (vv. 9–10). The contemporary hymn writer David Preston (b. 1939) exhorts us to use the psalms to praise God. He writes:

> There is nothing to compare with their blend of the subjective and the objective, the inner life and practical godliness, the knowledge of one's own rebellious heart and the knowledge of God.[5]

And the key verse may be verse 10 in which David states: 'And those who know your name put their trust in you, for you, O LORD, have not forsaken those who seek you.'

So as in Psalm 8—'How majestic is your name in all the earth'—we are brought back to what Gerald Wilson calls 'the theology of the divine "name" that permeates the whole Psalter.'[6] He continues: 'Those who "know the name" of Yahweh are the covenant people who have received the revelation of God's name and who therefore share an intimate relationship with him and faithfully serve him alone.' And this 'knowing' also is something from the heart—not just the head. Notice the three verbs of verse 10: know, trust, seek. Are all three evident in your daily walk with God?

But then at verse 13, the focus of the psalm changes from praise to prayer—prayer for deliverance (vv. 13–14), for justice (vv. 15–16), and finally for godless mankind to be put in his place (vv. 17–20). This final verse—'Let the nations know that they are but men!'—brings us full circle for Protagoras, Ralph Waldo Emerson and all those eminent philosophy professors were, in the end, 'but men.' As Charles Spurgeon writes on this verse: 'All the wisdom of Solomon, the power of Alexander [the Great], the eloquence of Demosthenes, if added together, would leave the possessor but a man.'[7]

In his New Testament letter, James reminds us of man's transience: 'What is your life? For you are a mist that appears for a little time and then vanishes' (Jas. 4:14). As I write this, the coronavirus is ravaging China, Egypt, Italy, the United States and Britain and mankind is reminded all too starkly of their mortality. In such troubled times, God has much to say to us through this little-known psalm. To the 'wicked . . . that forget God' (v. 17), God will come as judge—for 'he has established his throne in justice' (v. 7). But those who truly know him can say with the psalmist: 'You, O Lord, have never forsaken those who seek you.' (v. 10). Are you forgetting God, or knowing God?

> The Lord is king: tremble, O earth, and fear him,
> The God of heaven, by angel hosts adored;
> His people bow before him and revere him,
> So great and awesome: holy is the Lord!
>
> O Lord our God, you answered all who sought you:
> You punished sins, but sinners you restored;

Let all the nations worship and exalt you,
Proclaiming: holy is our God the Lord![8]

REFLECT ON THESE POINTS:

- David's thankful worship and praise is from the heart—indeed, 'with my whole heart'.
- Are you as determined as David that you 'will' give thanks, be glad, exult and sing praises to our great and merciful God?
- We praise and worship God because he is worthy of it and because glorifying God is 'the chief end of man.'

PSALM 10

Their cry goes up, 'How long?'

One advantage of studying the Bible in consecutive chapters is that you can't get away with missing out the difficult or more obscure bits, or the bits that are no-one's favourite. I would be staggered if any of my readers regarded Psalm 10 as their favourite psalm! But as it's *en route* from Psalm 9 to Psalm 11, here we are.

Many years ago whilst in Washington DC, I went out to Dulles Airport to meet a choir from a school in England who were doing a short tour of the eastern United States. It was late March but with a stiff breeze from the south and abundant sunshine the temperature was up in the 80s (as they say over there). I met them again the next morning to give them a tour of downtown Washington. I knew that overnight the wind had swung round to a frigid northerly and dressed accordingly. They didn't, and came dressed in shorts and T-shirts. It snowed! It was a shock! And from the generally optimistic tone of Psalm 9, the opening verse of Psalm 10 is a bit of a shock, especially as many commentators suggest that these two were originally one psalm. But moving from God's putting mankind in fear of him (Ps. 9:19–20) straight to 'Why, O Lord, do you stand far away? Why do you hide yourself in times of trouble?' is a shock. But if we're honest, we've all been there. Haven't you seen the cheat, the bully, the liar win, get all the best jobs, earn far more than you, marry some super-model and live in a house in which yours would fit multiple times and echoed—or at least thought—these questions of the psalmist?

The question that the psalmist asks—'How long?'—is one that David asked in Psalm 6. And it's all a question of perspective. Because God delays, the wicked presume—wrongly and foolishly—that 'There is no God' (v. 4), that 'God has forgotten', and that God has 'hidden his face and will never see it' (v. 11). Neither do they seem to perceive the obvious contradiction between the first statement and the other two. Their life exhibits an array of unattractive traits including pride (v. 4), insolence (vv. 4 and 11), deceit (v. 7) and violence (vv. 8–10), and yet also appear to enjoy both prosperity (v. 5) and security (v. 6). So both by their beliefs and their lifestyle, such folk show contempt for God and other human beings whom they mistreat appallingly. Thus, as one commentator puts it, 'one major concern of the psalmist appears to be revealed: the oppression of the defenceless people by the wicked, who deny the effective existence of God and forsake their divinely given role of extending God's care to the world in order to exploit and oppress those weaker than themselves.'[1]

What we have in the first half of Psalm 10 (vv. 2–11) is a description of the practical atheist. Later in the Psalter, we'll meet the theoretical atheist—the one who simply says, 'There is no God' (see Ps. 14:1 and 53:1). But the practical atheist, as James Boice calls them, is different. He, or she, 'is not concerned so much with the theoretical question as to the existence of God; rather they live and behave *as if* God does not exist.'[2] This is the person of whom this psalmist says, 'All his thoughts are, "There is no God"' (v. 4), literally 'there is no place for God in his schemes.' So I am bound to ask, 'Is this you?' Do you live your daily life *as if* God doesn't exist—he just has no place at all in your plans, your morals, your speech, or your treatment of others whether that be your spouse, your business associates, your neighbours, or the person in the street? And if it does, the psalmist would want you to know that contrary to appearance, you're skating on thin ice. So read on!

Do you live your daily life *as if* God doesn't exist?

There's an almost certainly apocryphal story about rivalry between two farmers—one a Christian, the other an atheist. The atheist said to the other, 'You plant your crops and work your fields six days a week, taking Sundays off to worship your God, and I'll work seven days a week and we'll see, come the autumn, who gets the bigger crop!' Well, October came and when both crops were harvested the atheist's crop was bigger than the Christian's. 'So what do you say now?' the atheist farmer sneered. The

Christian farmer replied, 'God doesn't settle his accounts in October!' And the New Testament tells us how God would have replied. 'Fool! This night your soul is required of you, and the things you have prepared, whose will they be?' (Lk. 12:20). 'So is the one,' concluded Jesus, 'who lays up treasure for himself and is not rich towards God.'

So how does the godly man react to this? First, he asks God to act—to 'arise, lift up your hand' (v. 12) and 'call wickedness to account' (v. 15). Second, he reminds himself that God *does* see (v. 14) despite what the wicked think. There's a wonderful heartening contrast between the atheist's claim that God 'will *never* see' (v. 11) and the psalmist's confident rebuttal, 'But you *do* see! (v. 14). And the atheist will discover that stating an untruth doesn't make it true however often, however loudly and however sincerely you state it.

> The atheist will discover that stating an untruth doesn't make it true.

It's almost as if, after his early downcast mood, the psalmist is now warming to his theme, for now the psalmist begins to recount all the other things he knows that God does. 'The LORD is king forever and ever' (v. 16). And here's a tiny taster of a recurring them in the Psalter—of God as King. The next time we come across it, it will take centre stage in Psalm 24 with the five-times repeated phrase of God as 'the King of glory.' And it's a theme that resounds through the gospels, especially Matthew's, and right to the end of Scripture where we read of Christ, the Warrior Messiah, riding upon a white horse 'and on his robe and on his thigh he has a name written, King of kings and Lord of lords' (Rev. 19:16).

And in these final verses of Psalm 10, the psalmist reminds himself—and us—of what God does for his faithful people. He is 'the helper of the fatherless' (v. 14). And yet the Christian has an even more wonderful promise that through Christ we have been adopted as God's sons (Eph. 1:5) with all the rights and privileges of sonship. Then the psalmist reminds us that God will 'hear the desire of the afflicted,' that he will 'strengthen their heart' and 'incline [his] ear to do justice to the fatherless and the oppressed' (vv. 17–18). God *will* finally settle his accounts with mankind 'so that the man who is of the earth may strike terror no more' (v. 18). In the meantime, the godly man and woman should keep a divine and eternal perspective always in view. One hymn writer seems to encapsulate much of Psalm 10 with this verse when he writes of Christ's church:

> Though with a scornful wonder
> Men see her sore oppressed,
> By schisms rent asunder,
> By heresies distressed:
> Yet saints their watch are keeping,

Their cry goes up, 'How long?'
And soon the night of weeping
Shall be the morn of song.[3]

REFLECT ON THESE POINTS:

- The practical atheist 'is not concerned so much with the theoretical question as to the existence of God; rather they live and behave as if God does not exist.' (James Boice)
- The atheist will discover that stating an untruth doesn't make it true however often, however loudly and however sincerely you state it.
- The godly man and woman should keep a divine and eternal perspective always in view.

PSALM 11

Let not your hearts be troubled

Psalm 11 asks a big question: 'If the foundations are destroyed, what can the righteous do?' (v. 3). It's the kind of question David might have asked against the background of the events recorded in 1 Samuel 20–22. David is on the run from Saul and seeks refuge with Ahimelech the priest at Nob. But he's spotted there by Doeg, one of Saul's supporters, who tells the King that Ahimelech is sheltering David, giving him food and weapons. Saul summons Ahimelech who says that David had told him he was on an errand from Saul and that's why he had given him shelter and provisions. But Saul doesn't believe him and has Ahimelech killed along with 84 of his fellow priests. So here is the King of Israel killing the priests of God. So: 'if the foundations are destroyed, what can the righteous do?' And it's the kind of question you might ask when you see the Christian faith and Christian values openly attacked in the media, or in your workplace, your school—maybe even your family. It's what you might ask when you hear a Church of England Bishop say that because 'the vast majority of people under 35 not only think what we're saying [about same-sex relationships] is incomprehensible, but also that we're plain wrong and wicked' the church should say something different.[1]

Psalm 11 is a psalm of two halves. In verses 1–3, David asks 'What shall we do?' In verses 4–6, he asks 'Where should we look?' And as a postscript, verse 7 offers us the eternal perspective on the whole matter.[2] The text gives us no idea as to the exact circumstances that brought David to write this psalm. And maybe that's an advantage, because it means we can apply it to our own circumstances more easily.

The psalm begins with a bold statement: 'In the LORD I take refuge' (v. 1a), in fact it's probably better understood as 'In the LORD I *have taken* refuge.' That decision has already been taken. And it's at odds with the advice that is being offered by close friends who are telling David to, as it were, run for the hills. And David's reaction is, 'How can you say that?' 'How can you say to my soul, "Flee like a bird to your mountain"?' (v. 1b). But in giving David such advice, they're settling for the safe option, but not the right option. And we're often tempted to take the 'flee to the mountain' option. When we hear God's name being vilified, or God's people being mocked we either turn tail and run, or just try to disappear into the background and say nothing—or worse. Like David, we feel threatened by the weapons of the wicked (v. 2), shooting at us when we least expect it. So what *can* the righteous do?

And the answer is given in the second part of the psalm. As a little-known metrical version of this psalm puts it:

> In God I will trust, though my counsellors say,
> O flee as a bird to your mountain away;
> The wicked are strong and the righteous are weak,
> Foundations are shaken, yet God will I seek.[3]

So this second half begins with an equally bold statement as did the first half, but this time it's not about the psalmist taking refuge in God, but about God himself. 'The LORD is in his holy temple; the LORD's throne is in heaven' (v. 4a). So to what is David referring by God's 'holy temple'? The temple that his son Solomon built was not yet in existence. No! David is thinking of the temple of God in heaven from which the Almighty looks down upon 'the children of man' to 'test' them (v. 4b). David uses the same language in later psalms.[4] In the Hebrew, David does not use the word used in the Old Testament to refer to the temple that Solomon built, but the word that Isaiah uses in his vision of the Lord—whose 'robe filled *the temple*'—in Isaiah 6. And the temple is associated with God's holiness. By God's throne, David is reminding us of the King who will judge the wicked. And these two images go together,

By God's throne, David is reminding us of the King who will judge the wicked.

for it's because of God's utter holiness that he hates sin and must therefore judge it in righteousness and justice. We read in Psalm 10:11 that the wicked 'says in his heart, "God has forgotten, he has hidden his face, he will never see it."' And here in Psalm 11:4b we discover just how wrong they are, for God's 'eyes see, his eyelids test the children of men.' The book of Proverbs reminds us: 'The eyes of the LORD are in every place, keeping watch on the evil and the good' (15:3).

In verse 5, we are told what this all-seeing, holy King will do—to the righteous and to the wicked. First, he 'tests' or 'examines' (NIV) the righteous. The Hebrew word has connotations of testing precious metals to see whether or not they are genuine. As Charles Spurgeon explains: 'God doth not hate them, but only tries them. They are precious to him, and therefore he refines them with afflictions. None of his children may hope to escape trial, nor indeed in our right minds would any of us desire to do so, for trial is the channel of many blessings.'[5] Is that how you look on the various trials God sends you? As I write this, my dear wife Sue has been undergoing treatment for two years for cancer. Physically she is quite weak, but spiritually she is still allowing God to test and refine her as he prepares her for her call to Glory.

But he also prepares judgement for the wicked whom 'his soul *hates*' because they '*love* violence' (v. 5). And the judgement of verse 6 sounds fearful. But this is not the

75

language of some frightening fairy tale, it's frighteningly real. Think Sodom and Gomorrah at Genesis 18:32! And don't be fooled by those who would try to convince you that this is just 'the God of the Old Testament.' The writer to the Hebrews in the New Testament warns us that not only is it 'a fearful thing to fall into the hands of the living God' (10:31) but that also 'our God is a consuming fire' (12:29). This is the God of the whole Bible!

As the psalm closes, David adds a kind of postscript with an eternal perspective as faith answers fear to produce hope and we, with the psalmist, look forward to seeing the very face of God. So, as the apostle Paul bids us, 'we do not lose heart. Though our outer self is wasting away, our inner self is being renewed day by day. For this light momentary affliction is preparing for us an eternal weight of glory beyond all comparison, as we look not to the things that are seen but to the things that are unseen. For the things that are seen are transient, but the things that are unseen are eternal' (2 Cor. 4:16–18). And for the Christian, seeing God's face is not wishful thinking, for this is what the apostle John would have us fix our eyes on: 'Beloved, we are God's children now, and what we will be has not yet appeared; but we know that when he appears we shall be like him, because we shall see him as he is' (1 Jn. 3:2). Those clothed in the righteousness of Christ really will see God's face! Now there's a perspective to hold on to.

Let not your hearts be troubled, you who believe
   in him;
Let not your faith be shaken, nor your hope
   burn dim.
Look to your risen Saviour, God's ever-living Word!
Soon from the throne of heaven comes our
   conquering Lord![6]

REFLECT ON THESE POINTS:

- When we hear God's name being vilified, or God's people being mocked, do we either turn tail and run, or just try to disappear into the background and say nothing—or worse?
- 'None of God's children may hope to escape trial, nor indeed in our right minds would any of us desire to do so, for trial is the channel of many blessings.' (Charles Spurgeon)
- Faith answers fear to produce hope and we, with the psalmist, look forward to seeing the very face of God.

PSALM 12

For we have no help but Thee

I have often thought that one of the saddest, most unlikable characters in the Bible is Peninnah who makes her sole appearance in the opening verses of 1 Samuel. We know only three things about her: she was one of the two wives of Elkanah, the other being Hannah; she had many children; she repeatedly taunted Hannah for her childlessness.

> Now [Elkanah] used to go up year by year from his city to worship and to sacrifice to the Lord of hosts at Shiloh ... On the day when Elkanah sacrificed, he would give portions to Peninnah his wife and to all her sons and daughters. But to Hannah he gave a double portion, because he loved her, though the Lord had closed her womb. And her rival used to provoke her grievously to irritate her, because the Lord had closed her womb. So it went on year by year (1 Sam. 1:3–7).

How utterly heartless and cruel. And what an indictment to have all those children, a loving and godly husband, and yet to get one's pleasure from taunting someone else— not just once, but year after year. How truly James writes in his New Testament epistle: 'The tongue is a fire, a world of unrighteousness' (Jas. 3:6).

The evil of the tongue has been a recurring theme in these opening psalms. Even in the first eleven psalms, we have come across spoken revolt against God (2:2–3), lies (4:2; 5:6; 7:14), flattery (5:9), boasting (10:3, 6, 11, 13), mischief, cursing and deceit (10:7). And the sins of the tongue reach a crescendo in Psalm 12 with what one commentator calls 'empty talk, smooth talk and double talk' and much else besides.[1] What havoc the tongue wreaks. It breaks up homes, divides families, sends the innocent to prison, crushes hearts, disrupts churches and maybe sends some to an early grave.

Like its predecessor, Psalm 12 is a plea to God for help when evil—and especially evil-speaking—is rife and the godly are suffering under its weight. The opening word— 'save', or 'help'—is like the shout of a drowning person. And David then states his case in hyperbole to give it full force, so desperate is he. The godly folk, says David, have 'gone', they have 'vanished' (v. 1)—literally they've disappeared. The prophets of Israel wrote and spoke at times in much the same way. 'The godly has perished from the earth, and there is no one upright among mankind,' wrote the prophet Micah (7:2). And it all sounds reminiscent of Elijah when he complained to God that 'I, even I only, am left, and they seek my life, to take it away' (1 Kgs. 19:10). Elijah was mistaken and maybe David was too. It just seemed as if the godly had gone. And don't you sometimes feel the same—in the family, the workplace, the school, the pub, the party? Do you feel as if you're the only one not using the Son of God's name as an expletive, the only one who believes what the Bible says? And, like David, it may be more than that—you may be the subject of the lies that are spread as a consequence. Then use David's prayer: 'Save me, O Lord!'

In verse 2, we hear more detail of the verbal battering David is facing. First there are the lies. How easily they appear from our mouths—things that we know are just plain wrong and dishonest. And if we know our Bibles, we know it's displeasing to God. 'Lying lips are an abomination to the Lord,' we read in Proverbs 12:20. Then there is flattery—literally 'smooth talk.' In a later psalm we shall read of the one whose 'speech was smooth as butter, yet has he war in his heart' (Ps. 55:21). And thirdly, there are those who speak with 'a double heart'—literally 'they speak with a heart and heart'! They say one thing, but what they really mean is hidden, so to speak, in the other heart. Here's how Martin Luther paraphrased part of this psalm:

> They teach a cunning, false and fine,
> In their own wits they found it;
> Their heart to truth is not inclined,
> Nor on God's Word well-grounded.

One chooses this, another that;
Strife and division they create,
And yet make pious pretence.[2]

I'm reminded of the Pharisees who come to Jesus to try and catch him out with the one about paying taxes to Caesar, but their opening line is: 'Teacher, we know that you speak and teach rightly and show no partiality, but truly teach the way of God . . .' (Lk. 20:21). Butter speech and warring hearts! And if you're the victim, then use David's prayer: 'Save me, O LORD.' If you're the perpetrator, then beware lest your victim is praying David's second prayer: 'May the LORD cut off all flattering lips, the tongue that makes great boasts' (v. 3).

Just when you think you can't take any more of this litany of evil words, a different voice altogether is heard.

But just when you think you can't take any more of this litany of evil words, a different voice altogether is heard. God speaks (v. 5)—the first time we have heard his voice directly since the second psalm—as he steps in to assume 'his kingly role as protector of the defenceless.'[3] And with wonderful irony, God offers his answer to the boast of the previous verse: 'those who say, "With our tongue we will prevail, our lips are with us; who is master over us?"' God answers with a magisterial, 'I am.'

Lest we should miss the stark contrast between the lies, the flattering and the boasting of verses 2–4, and God's spoken intervention in verse 5, David offers us a commentary: 'The words of the LORD are pure words, like silver tried in a furnace of earth, purified seven times. (v. 6, NKJV). When Elizabeth II was crowned Queen in Westminster Abbey on 2 June 1953, the Moderator of the General Assembly of the Church of Scotland, James Pitt-Watson, handed her a copy of the Bible, describing it as 'the most valuable thing this world affords.' The question for us, therefore, is, 'Will we respond to hearing the very Word of God as David does in this psalm?' David's response is in verse 7. David has heard what God has said, and for him, that settles it. God has promised to keep his people in safety so, decides David: 'You shall keep them, O LORD, You shall preserve them from this generation forever' (v. 7, NKJV). And you need to notice how the psalm ends. 'On every side the wicked prowl, as vileness is exalted among the children of men' (v. 8). The evil speakers are still strutting their stuff out there. But, as the apostle Paul will remind us, 'If God is for us, who can be against us?' (Rom. 8:31). No-one of any eternal consequence.

> Lead us, heavenly Father, lead us
> O'er the world's tempestuous sea;
> Guard us, guide us, keep us, feed us,
> For we have no help but Thee;

Yet possessing, every blessing
If our God our Father be.[4]

REFLECT ON THESE POINTS:

- What havoc the tongue wreaks. It breaks up homes, divides families, sends the innocent to prison, crushes hearts, disrupts churches and maybe sends some to an early grave.
- With wonderful irony, God offers his answer to the boast of 'those who say, "With our tongue we will prevail, our lips are with us; who is master over us?"' God answers with a magisterial, 'I am.'
- As the apostle Paul will remind us, 'If God is for us, who can be against us?' (Rom. 8:31). No-one of any eternal consequence.

PSALM 13

O love that wilt not let me go

In his book *The Message of Worship*, John Risbridger tells of the days just after the death of his and his wife Alison's son Daniel. He remembered how hard they found church-going—'because the hymnody of previous generations made space for lament; the church today rarely does.'[1] Well, if the latter part of that statement is true—and experience tells me it is—then modern hymnody does not reflect the Bible's songbook in which there are more psalms of lament than psalms of praise and thanksgiving. That's why neither our acts of corporate worship nor our private devotions should neglect the regular singing or reading of the Psalms.

Psalm 13 is a wonderful psalm to know when you're feeling abandoned by God. It is stunningly honest in its portrayal of the godly person's thoughts under such trials, it sets out a tried and tested route to get us from the sorrowing (and worse) of verses 1 and 2 to the singing of verse 6, and it offers us some sound theology along the way. For what more could one ask in just six verses? It's also simple in its structure—three, two-verse stanzas—which gets the commentators alliterating, from Michael Wilcock's pain, prayer and praise, to Dale Ralph Davis's anguish, asking and assurance. So, three sections—but with some alliteration.

First, putting your questions to God (vv. 1–2). In Psalm 12, David used hyperbole to make his point. In Psalm 13, he uses repetition. 'How long?' he asks—not once, not twice, but four times—and they're all directed at God. Questioning God has a good biblical trail—Cain, Abraham and Moses come to mind.[2] But David's questions are not asked to illicit information from God, but rather to give voice to his deep misgivings about the character and activity—or rather lack of activity—of God and its devastating effect on his life. His first two questions are about God himself. 'How long? Will you forget me forever?' How long will you hide your face from me?' (v. 1). It's obvious that David's plight has been going on for some long time. And often that can itself be the root cause of our feeling abandoned by God. In the short term, we cope; we trust God's silence. As James Boice observes: 'It is different when the short-term experience becomes a long-term pattern, and we begin to wonder whether God's silence may endure "forever" . . . We begin to imagine that the end of this period of distressing and painful abandonment will never come.'[3] We struggle not so much with the sharpest as with the longest trials. But bereavement, illness, pain, fatigue, loneliness can all be at the root of feeling abandoned and rejected by God, of feeling that God no longer blesses you—that he 'hides his face' from you. And if this is your state, then follow David's example: begin by asking God your questions—humbly, yet honestly.

Putting your questions to God is a good place to start, but then (vv. 3–4) pray your worries to God—as the old hymn teaches us, 'Take it to the LORD in prayer.'[4] Notice how this is the turning point for David. His focus is still on his trials, but he's now praying to the God whom he has just suggested had forgotten about him. God is still the immortal, invisible God you know him to be; he has not forgotten you.

Putting your questions to God is a good place to start, but then pray your worries to God.

In verse 4, David seems to plead for God's reputation's sake to come to his aid—lest David's enemies think that they can triumph over the one who trusts in God. That's what Moses did when God announced that he would destroy the children of Israel because of their golden calf idolatry. And Moses pleads with God, saying that if God were to do that then the Egyptians would say, 'With evil intent did [God] bring them out, to kill them in the mountains and to consume them from the face of the earth' (Exodus 32:12). 'Do this, O God, for your reputation's sake,' is a wonderful way for a Christian to pray.

And having first put your questions to God, and second prayed your worries to God, now finally, says David, put your trust in God (vv. 5–6). So why the dramatic change?

Well it's not because David has taken a deep breath, or had a cup of tea, or 'pulled himself together.' And it's not mere wishful thinking. David's trust—and your trust—needs to have firm foundations, theological foundations, and for David there are three. 'But I have trusted in your steadfast love,' says David at the start of verse 5. The NIV may be right to put this statement in the present tense: 'I trust.' But it's God's 'steadfast love' that we need to focus upon. Different Bible versions use different words to translate the Hebrew word *hesed*,[5] but however you translate it, this is one of the central theological themes of the Old Testament—and certainly of the psalms. There are over 120 uses of the word in the psalms; over one-third of the psalms contain the word at least once. So it's important we understand what it means.

> **David's trust—and your trust—needs to have firm foundations, theological foundations.**

The most literal translation of the word would be 'loyal love' or 'covenant love.' God uses the word to describe himself. As God descends in the cloud atop Mount Sinai for the giving of the law a second time, we read:

> The LORD passed before [Moses] and proclaimed,
> 'The LORD, the LORD, a God merciful and gracious,
> slow to anger, and abounding in *steadfast love* and
> faithfulness (Exodus 34:6, emphasis added).

So God here describes himself as 'abounding in steadfast love' towards Israel. And that in itself is an extraordinary miracle of grace. For what have the children of Israel just done? They've just persuaded Aaron to make the golden calf and have committed apostasy and rebellion against God! They'd worshipped the idol in the very shadow of Sinai. So whenever you read *hesed* always remember that it also has overtones of amazing grace. As Dale Ralph Davis puts it: 'It is not merely love but loyal love, not merely kindness but dependable kindness.'[6] This is 'the love that wilt not let me go.' So that's what convinces David—and should convince us—that God has not forgotten us. He never will. He never can.

But there's more. Not only is David encouraged by God's loyal-love, but his heart 'rejoices in [God's] salvation.' Of course, David's understanding of salvation wasn't as fully developed spiritually as is ours. The great Old Testament depiction of God as saviour is, of course, the exodus and the rescue of his people from the bondage of Egyptian slavery. But to us, that merely signposts forward to Christ's rescue of his people from the bondage of sin. We have even more reason to 'rejoice in our salvation' than did David.

Finally, David looks back and remembers God's great faithfulness to him in the past. He counts his blessings and remembers that 'God has dealt bountifully' with him (v. 6). That puts a song on David's lips, and it should do so on ours. So, yes, ask God your questions, turn your worries into prayers, but then remember all that God has done for you—and sing for joy!

> O love, that wilt not let me go,
> I rest my weary soul in Thee;
> I give Thee back the life I owe,
> That in Thine ocean depths its flow
> May richer, fuller be.[7]

REFLECT ON THESE POINTS:

- We struggle not so much with the sharpest as with the longest trials. But bereavement, illness, pain, fatigue, loneliness can all be at the root of feeling abandoned and rejected by God, of feeling that God no longer blesses you—that he 'hides his face' from you.
- 'Do this, O God, for your reputation's sake,' is a wonderful way for a Christian to pray.
- This is 'the love that wilt not let me go.' So that's what convinces David—and should convince us—that God has not forgotten us. He never will. He never can.

PSALM 14

Perverse and foolish

There's an apocryphal story of a teenage girl at a boarding school writing home to her parents, and the letter reads:

> Dear Mummy and Daddy, You need to know that last night the boarding house where I sleep caught fire. Some of the other girls died. But I was rescued by this lovely young fireman—and we decided to elope. We're now engaged and plan to get married very soon. With love from your daughter, Amy.
> PS: None of the above is true, but I have just failed my GCSE mocks but you do need to keep things in proportion.

Well Psalm 14 is the kind of psalm in which you discover, not that things aren't as bad as you first feared, but they're much worse! For here we read God's verdict on humankind as he 'looks down from heaven on the children of man' (v. 2). And his verdict is devastating, and there aren't any let-out clauses. The psalm can best be read in three stanzas: human folly (vv. 1–3); God's judgement (vv. 4–6); a hope of restoration (v. 7).

The last time we heard the wicked speak was in Psalm

12:4 where they asked the rhetorical question, 'Who is master over us?' Here, as it were, in Psalm 14:1 they answer their question with the—false—assumption that 'There is no God.' But, as Derek Kidner, astutely points out, this assertion 'is treated in Scripture not as a sincere if misguided conviction, but as an irresponsible gesture of defiance' against God. And God refers to such as 'the fool,' and in Scripture's wisdom literature folly is the opposite of wisdom. We're also told that the fool makes this declaration 'in his heart' (v. 1) which in this context means his will. So this declaration about God is not an off-the-cuff thought, it's a definite act of will. And that act of will shapes both their character—'they are corrupt'—and their actions, which are 'abominable' or vile (NIV). This blockbuster of an opening verse then ends with this stunning assertion, that 'there is none who does good.' And verse 3 repeats that truth 'there is none who does good,' and just to make sure we get the point adds, 'not even one.'

Now I'm reckoning that some of my readers might raise an eyebrow at this point—maybe two eyebrows: 'No-one does good, not even one?' Surely this is as unlikely as the one about Amy and the fireman! 'After all,' you might say, 'I know a lot of people who do a lot of good.' Yes, but you're looking at this from the human perspective, and verse 2 makes it very clear that what we have here is *God's* perspective. And from God's perspective, 'all our righteous deeds are like a polluted garment' (Is. 64:6). To illustrate this, James Boice tells the story—again possibly apocryphal—of the American Vietnam POW who had spent his time in prison winning at Monopoly. Upon returning home, he went to his local bank. When asked by the teller how much he wanted to deposit, he replied, 'Just over half-a-million dollars!' producing his large envelope of monopoly money. Says Boice: 'Human righteousness is like monopoly money. It has its uses in the "game" we call life, but it is not real currency, and it does not work in God's domain. God requires *divine* righteousness.'[1] That's what the apostle Paul means when he writes to the Romans of those who 'being ignorant of the righteousness of God, and seeking to establish their own, they did not submit to God's righteousness' (Rom. 10:3).

Indeed, Paul uses these very verses (Ps. 14:1–3) as he concludes his argument—which runs from Romans 1:18 to 3:20—of the sinfulness of each human being. He tells us that we 'did not see fit to acknowledge God' (Rom. 1:28), that 'all are under sin' (3:9) for 'as it is written: "None is righteous, no, not one; no one understands; no one seeks for God"' (3:10–11). In other words, the apostle is repeating the truths of the psalmist that 'no one unaided by the Spirit of God: has any righteousness by which to lay a claim upon God; has any true understanding of God; or seeks God.'[2]

Then in verses 4–6 God gives his judgement. The

callous sins of the evildoers—they devour God's people with no more thought than they would give to eating a piece of bread (v. 4)—will result in their being terrified (v. 5). This sounds as if the biter is bitten. For it was only a pay back in our Bibles that these folk were 'striking terror' themselves (Ps. 10:18). Now the terrifying are to be terrified. And all because whilst the evildoers 'do not call upon the LORD' (v. 4), the righteous find that 'the LORD is [their] refuge' (v. 6).

Whilst the evildoers 'do not call upon the LORD', the righteous find that 'the LORD is [their] refuge'.

But all this leaves us with a bit of a conundrum which, whilst I'm tempted to ignore it, I feel we shouldn't. For if there is 'none who does good, not even one' (v. 3), then who are 'my people' (v. 4) and 'the generation [or company, NIV] of the righteous' in verse 5? Where did they come from? Well, just as one might say that although the name of God never appears in the book of Esther, yet the whole book is underwritten by the sovereignty of God, so one could say that although the word doesn't appear in Psalm 14, the assumptions of verses 4–7 are underwritten by the grace of God. Do you see, we've all been there: 'there is none who does good, not even one.' We must all sing those words of the well-known hymn, 'Perverse and foolish oft I strayed.'[3]

… But God, being rich in mercy, because of the
great love with which he loved us, even when we
were dead in our trespasses, made us alive together
with Christ—by grace you have been saved
(Eph. 2:4–5).

Or to continue that verse of the hymn:

Perverse and foolish oft I strayed,
But yet in love He sought me,
And on His shoulder gently laid,
And home rejoicing brought me.[4]

Which leads us to the third and final part of the psalm—
verse 7—as the psalmist, possibly at a later time, adds a
kind of postscript doxology, looking forward to a time
when 'salvation' will come 'for Israel out of Zion' and
'when the LORD restores the fortunes of his people,' to a
time of rejoicing and gladness for God's chosen people.
The psalmist and his contemporaries could sing these
words looking forward to the promised salvation, in the
Hebrew 'yeshua' from which word the name of our Saviour
comes—'Jesus, for he will save his people from their
sins' (Matt. 1:21). And we can sing them looking forward
to Christ's Second Advent 'when the Lord restores the
fortunes of his people' which will be the completion of
this great salvation. Let our prayer be in these words of
Martin Luther:

Defend Thy truth, O God, and stay
This evil generation;
And from the error of its way
Keep Thine own congregation.
The wicked everywhere abound
And would Thy little flock confound;
But Thou art our salvation![5]

REFLECT ON THESE POINTS:

- From God's perspective, 'all our righteous deeds are like a polluted garment' (Is. 64:6).
- 'Human righteousness is like monopoly money. It has its uses in the 'game' we call life, but it is not real currency, and it does not work in God's domain. God requires divine righteousness.' (James Boice)

PSALM 15

Take time to be holy

Psalms 14 and 15 could hardly have two more different opening verses. Psalm 14 opens with 'the fool' who 'says in his heart "There is no God,"' someone who is 'corrupt' and does 'abominable deeds.' Here in Psalm 15, David is concerned about personal holiness—the conditions under which mankind may dwell with God. The two psalms together echo those two people on two different paths going to two very different destinies with which the Psalter began.

Psalm 15 breaks into three unequal parts—the question (v. 1), the answer (vv. 2–5a) and the affirmation (v. 5b).[1] The question of verse 1 is truly *the* big question. In our school days great importance is placed on knowing the right answers—especially on the examination day. But in adulthood, we realise that better than knowing the right answers is the wisdom to ask the right questions. And this *is* the right question to ask: 'O LORD, who shall sojourn in your tent? Who shall dwell on your holy hill?' It's likely that David's contemporaries would have heard the words about God's 'tent' and 'holy hill' as references to the event recorded in 2 Samuel 6 when David brought up the ark of the Lord to Jerusalem—God's holy hill—and 'set it in its place, inside *the tent* that David had pitched for it' (2 Sam. 6:17). Some commentators take David's question to refer to coming to worship God, and although that might in a limited sense be the case, the words 'sojourn' and 'dwell' are not words that refer to a brief visit—to worship God, as it were. So I think we're nearer the mark to take this as, 'Lord, who can live with you in heaven?' Psalm 14 made reference to 'the generation of the righteous' (v. 5) and to God's people (v. 7) and now David is asking, as it were, 'Lord, who are these people?' It's a good question to ask.

Before we consider the answer that David gives, we should notice the answer he *doesn't* give. There's nothing here about doing religious things. It's not about what you do on Sundays, about 'worship' in the narrow sense. It's about who you are, your relationships, your money and your heart—about what John Stott calls 'social holiness.'[2] We also need to understand that the answer is a *representative* list, not an all-inclusive one. David asks a very similar question in Psalm 24:3 and although the answer he offers there is similar (Ps. 24:4–6), it's not identical. The same can be said of Isaiah 33:14b–16.

The answer comes under four headings alternating between positives and negatives. David begins with the one who 'walks blamelessly and does what it right, and speaks the truth from his heart' (v. 2). Blamelessness does not mean sinless perfection but speaks of integrity, of living a godly life. It's what God commanded of Abram when he said, 'Walk before me, and be blameless' (Gen. 17:1). It's the way Paul describes the Christian's lifestyle when he writes. that God chose us in Christ 'that we should be holy and blameless before him' (Eph. 1:4). It's having a life that matches your faith. The American Christian businessman of the last century Marion Wade (1898–1973) popularised the motto: 'If you don't live it, you don't believe it!' And integrity will show itself by doing what is right and speaking only what is true (v. 2).

Integrity will show itself by doing what is right and speaking only what is true.

The second group of traits has to do with our treatment of friends and neighbours in what is a clear echo of God's instructions to his people to 'love your neighbour as yourself' (Lev. 19:18). This group is in the negative: no slander, no evil deeds, no back biting. We've heard so much in the earlier psalms about the immense damage wrought by the liars, the boastful, the flatterers, the deceitful— those unwilling to control their tongues. This cannot be true of the person who would 'dwell on [God's] holy hill.'

The third group concerns the company we keep and don't keep, as well as whom we admire and seek to model our lives upon and whom we deplore and refuse to follow. A character in one of Joseph Conrad's novels states correctly that 'You shall judge of a man by his foes as well as by his friends.'[3] Who do you most admire? Who is it you seek to model your life upon? And what is your attitude towards those who are God's people? Do you truly 'honour those who fear the Lord' (v. 4), or do you more often criticise them, talk about them behind their back, even poke fun at them? The more you grow to love God, the more you will grow to love the people of God—and to despise the ways, the lifestyles and the attitudes of the ungodly world around you. I'm not advocating that we cut ourselves off from anyone who does not profess a living faith in the Lord Jesus Christ. Indeed, we cannot love our neighbours if we won't even speak with them or try to develop cordiality with them. But beware when you find yourself wanting to 'keep up with the Joneses' when you know that the Joneses don't keep up with God! The people you admire are a litmus test of your heart.

The people you admire are a litmus test of your heart.

Fourthly, David turns to promise-keeping, for the godly person is the one for whom their word is their bond. It's easy to keep our promises when keeping them is cost free. But what do we do when circumstances change and we suddenly realise that keeping a promise is going to cost us dearly? Finally, there is the issue of money—as one commentator puts it, that 'for the godly, people are more important than money.'[4]

In the third section of the psalm, we have the final affirmation: 'He who does these things shall never be moved' (v. 5b). So how do you live up to 'these things'? And if, like me, your answer is 'Terribly!' then what to do? There are two responses we need to avoid. The first is that of reading Psalm 15 and saying, 'Okay, I just need to pull up my socks and try harder.' But you'll never succeed. No ordinary human being ever has. But the Lord Jesus Christ did and when we come to him in repentance and faith, he forgives us all our sin, and that's how we may dwell with God for eternity. But here's the second mistake we can make, and that is to stop at that point, as if what David says in Psalm 15 no longer matters. But it does, as John Stott clearly points out.

> No one has perfectly fulfilled this ideal except the man Christ Jesus. He alone has entered the presence of God in heaven in virtue of his own merit. For us, access to God is possible only through Christ. But, having been brought near to God by Christ, we can enjoy continuing fellowship with him only if by his grace we lead the kind of holy life which this psalm depicts.'[5]

Some preachers are so keen that we don't take the 'must try harder' option that they leave us with the impression that, for the Christian, living a holy life no longer matters.

Holiness does matter. We need, in the words of the old hymn, to 'take time to be holy.'

> Take time to be holy, be calm in your soul;
> Each thought and each temper beneath his control.
> Thus led by His Spirit and filled with His love,
> You soon shall be fitted for service above.[6]

Reflect on these points:

- There's nothing here about doing religious things. It's not about what you do on Sundays, about 'worship' in the narrow sense. It's about who you are, your relationships, your money and your heart—about what John Stott calls 'social holiness.'
- Beware when you find yourself wanting to 'keep up with Joneses' when you know that the Joneses don't keep up with God! The people you admire are a litmus test of your heart.
- 'No one has perfectly fulfilled this ideal except the man Christ Jesus' (John Stott).

PSALM 16

Blessed Assurance

We don't know the particular circumstances that surrounded David when he wrote this psalm but what we know of David's life is that trouble, sorrow and hardship were never far away. And our lives, even as God's covenant people, are no different. And in this psalm, we can see three ways in which our lives should relate to God.

First, we should share David's commitment to God (vv. 1–4). David makes only one request to God in the whole psalm and it's in verse 1: 'Preserve me, O God, for in you I take refuge.' David is asking God to keep watch over him, just like David in his days as a shepherd watched over, provided refuge for, his sheep. What do children do when they awake afraid at night? They run to their parents' room—and in the same way David runs to God, and he bids us do the same. Now just think about it. This is the David of whom we read in 1 Samuel 17 that as a shepherd he had killed lions and bears in order to protect his sheep. And later in the same chapter, David goes out to kill Goliath. So committing yourself to God does not make you a wimp! Indeed, it often takes courage to trust God and not yourself.

And David gives us two reasons why we should commit

ourselves to God: first, because 'You are my Lord'; and second because 'I have no good thing apart from [God].' And if both of those truths are truly embedded in our hearts, what a difference it will make to the way we live our lives each day. Which raises two questions that we need to answer. First, 'Is God your Lord?' Have you truly committed your whole life—for time and for eternity—to him? And second, 'Do you truly believe that there's no good gift that doesn't come from God?' In James 1:17 we read, 'Every good and perfect gift is from above, coming down from the Father of the heavenly lights, who does not change like shifting shadows.' This was David's God, but is he *your* God? Are you, like David here in Psalm 16, committed to God?

Second, we should share David's contentment in God (vv. 5–8). Henry Blunt (1794–1843)—an evangelical Anglican minister of the early nineteenth century—in a sermon on the Children of Israel's grumbling to God in Numbers 11, wrote:

> What a lesson we might learn on spiritual contentment from a certain shepherd on Salisbury Plain. When asked, 'What weather are we likely to have today?' he replied, 'It will be what pleases me.' When asked how he could be so confident of that, he replied: 'Because it will be what pleases God, and what pleases God shall please me.'[1]

That's contentment in God—that what pleases God, pleases me, that whatever God sends into your life, you will still find contentment. And what is the source of David's contentment in God? Verse 5, because *God* has assigned his 'portion and cup'; because *God* has 'made his lot secure' (NIV).

But there's more. David writes in verse 6: 'The lines have fallen for me in pleasant places; indeed, I have a beautiful inheritance.' And here we have echoes of Joshua dividing the land, as Moses had allocated it, between the twelve tribes after the conquest of Canaan. Each tribe had its own portion, its own lot or inheritance to be passed down through the generations. But then we read in Joshua 13:33: 'But to the tribe of Levi,' that is the priestly tribe, 'Moses gave no inheritance; the LORD, the God of Israel is *their inheritance*, just as he said to them.' And Asaph picks up the same thought in Psalm 73 where we read (v. 26): 'My flesh and my heart may fail, but God is the strength of my heart and *my portion* forever.' And if David can describe *his* inheritance as 'beautiful', how much more the Christian believer. For the apostle Peter writes of 'An inheritance [there's that word again!] that is imperishable, and undefiled and unfading, kept in heaven for you' (1 Pet. 1:4).

> **That's contentment in God— that what pleases God, pleases me.**

And so as we read David's psalm with Christian eyes, we're reminded that the inheritance that we have in our Lord Jesus Christ is not land, or money, or property—it's God himself! That's the greatest gift that God gives us. And that if I have God then I have everything I will ever need—for life, for death, for eternity! No wonder David goes on in verses 7–8 to praise God—for his counsel, for his instruction (available day or night) and his ever-presence. And that's the basis, the foundation, undergirding David's statement at the end of verse 8 that 'I shall not be shaken.' That's the outworking of his godly contentment.

Finally, we should share David's confidence in God (vv. 9–11). Now these last three verses have been made famous because Peter preaches Christ's resurrection from them in his Pentecost sermon in Acts 2. But we must be careful not to make David say more than he actually does. Peter himself in his first letter explains how the Old Testament writers didn't fully understand to what the Spirit of Christ within them was referring when predicting Christ's sufferings and subsequent glory. So David is not here making a conscious prophecy of Jesus' resurrection. But these are God-breathed verses about the conquest of death and the fullness of life and joy in the presence of God which would be fulfilled, not because of David, but because of David's greater Son, the Lord Jesus Christ.

And if today you are trusting in Christ, then you can have that same confidence when you come to face death.

For we believe on the basis of God's character and God's Word that he will not abandon us to the grave. That's why the apostle Paul can write, 'For the trumpet will sound, and the dead will be raised imperishable, and we shall all be changed' (1 Cor. 15:52). Or as David puts it in here Psalm 16:

> You have made known to me the path of life;
> in your presence there is fullness of joy;
> at your right hand are pleasures for evermore (v. 11).

So just as death was not the end for the Messiah to whom these verses look forward in prophetic anticipation, so if you are a believer, death is not the end, but rather the beginning of an eternity in the presence of God. In the meantime, for the Christian—as for everyone—the insecurities of life don't just disappear, but we're empowered in Christ to walk with him in that 'path of life' of which David speaks, through whatever dangers and trials we are facing. Thus based on the commitment of our lives to God, the contentment that we find in him and the confidence that we can, through faith, have in him, we can say with the psalmist: 'I have set the LORD always before me. Because he is at my right hand, I shall not be shaken' (v. 8).

> Blessed assurance, Jesus is mine:
> O what a foretaste of glory divine!
> Heir of salvation, purchase of God,
> Born of His Spirit, washed in His blood.

This is my story, this is my song,
Praising my Saviour all the day long.[2]

REFLECT ON THESE POINTS:

- 'Do you truly believe that there's no good gift that doesn't come from God?
- That's contentment in God—that 'what pleases God, pleases me,' that whatever God sends into your life, you will still find contentment.
- The inheritance that we have in our Lord Jesus Christ is not land, or money, or property—it's God himself! That's the greatest gift that God gives us.

PSALM 17

I have a Friend

ere is a rarity in the Psalter—a psalm that is entitled as 'A Prayer'. There are only four and you won't meet another until Psalm 86. (For the curious, the other two are 90 and 142.) So it has at least two strands of teaching— that even in the greatest calamities of life we can depend upon our covenant-honouring God, as well as teaching us how to pray. Like Psalm 16, this psalm also has a profound last sentence which we shall want to ponder carefully. Although there's nothing in the psalm's title to give its historical setting, a number of commentators suggest that its background is in the events of 1 Samuel 23 when Saul is in deadly pursuit of David. But Saul is miraculously called away when a messenger comes saying, 'Hurry and come, for the Philistines have made a raid against the land' (1 Sam. 23:27). There's divine providence for you! And as David makes his plea to God for protection and deliverance, he pleads four things to God. It's a pattern we might adapt in our own times of distress.

First, David pleads his innocence (vv. 1–5). In essence, he's adopting the description of the godly life of which we read in the two previous psalms. Now we mustn't read more into David than he means. He's not claiming sinless perfection. Imagine you're in a courtroom. The charge has been read out and the Judge asks you: 'How do you plead, guilty or not guilty?' And knowing that you are, you reply, 'Not guilty.' Now you're not claiming never to have done anything wrong in your life, but only in regard to these specific charges. This is David's position. He's saying that he's innocent of the false charges his enemies are making against him. His is 'a just cause' (v. 1). He wants 'vindication' as God's 'eyes behold the right' (v. 2). Indeed, he knows that God already knows this because God has 'tried' and 'tested' his heart (v. 3)—both words have overtones of metallurgy. As one commentator states, God will 'find no dross in his life.'[1] It's good to have a clear conscience before God.

Second, David pleads God's character (vv. 6–9). This is a wonderful thing to do in our prayers. The particular attribute of God that David pleads is his 'steadfast love' (v. 7). David loves God's steadfast love! We heard him on the same subject in Psalm 13: 'But I have trusted in your steadfast love' he wrote (Ps. 13:5). This is God's covenant-keeping, promise-keeping, loyal, merciful love, and David is therefore confident to base his plea for God's protection and deliverance upon it. It's as if David is saying: 'God has kept his promises in the past, God is unchanging, so he will keep them again now.' And as well as the many Old Testament promises that David had, we also have some truly wonderful New Testament promises of God's steadfast love that were unknown to David. Read them, know them, claim them!

And what may be less obvious at first reading is that David is also making Scripture the basis of his prayer, and that's another wonderful thing to do as you pray. In verses 7 and 8 we find distinct echoes of Moses' Songs of Deliverance in Exodus 15 and Deuteronomy 32. Here in Psalm 17:7, David speaks of God 'wondrously showing' his 'steadfast love' and of saving David from his enemies 'at [more likely, by] your right hand.' Moses uses all three phrases—and in the Hebrew, they're identical—in Exodus 15:11–13. Then in verse 8, David uses these two lovely metaphors of God's protection: 'Keep me as the apple of your eye; hide me in the shadow of your wings.' And Moses talking of God's protection of Israel uses the same two pictures in Deuteronomy 32:10–12. But before you can claim Scripture, you need to know Scripture!

Thirdly, David pleads his present danger (vv. 10–14) as he tells God three things about his enemies. First, 'they close their heart to pity' (v. 10)—literally 'they are enclosed in their own fat'! What a picture! As Stewart Perowne comments: 'This may refer both to the outward condition and the state of their heart.'[2] Second, they speak arrogantly with their mouths (v. 10). We've had so much about the misuse of our tongues in these early psalms. Repetition is a good teaching technique. Clearly God thinks we need telling about this one more than once. Third, they have surrounded him, suggesting a determination to destroy him. David is clearly under severe attack, so when you feel life is closing in on you because of the words and actions of others, do what David did—'take it to the Lord in prayer' as the old hymn says.[3] David contemplates the ephemeral satisfaction that is the lot of the 'men of this world' (v. 14) which sets up the contrast for the final, eye-catching verse as fourthly and finally David pleads his future hope.

> As for me, I shall behold your face in
> righteousness;
> when I awake, I shall be satisfied with your likeness
> (v. 15).

The personal pronoun actually comes first in the Hebrew giving it the emphatic contrast with the verse before—'I in righteousness, I shall behold ...' And like Job in his much more famous 'In my flesh I shall see God' (Job 19:26), David places his hope on seeing God when he, as it were, awakes from death.

David places his hope on seeing God when he, as it were, awakes from death.

It's what Allan Harman calls 'a glimpse of eternity' in which David 'grasps something, however tenuous, of a doctrine of resurrection.'[4] Awaking from sleep is how resurrection is spoken about. Isaiah writes of how 'Your dead bodies

111

shall live; their bodies shall rise. You who dwell in the dust awake and sing for joy!' (Is. 26:19). Or this from Daniel: 'And many of those who sleep in the dust of the earth shall awake, some to everlasting life, and some to shame and everlasting contempt' (Dan. 12:2). So here we have a foretaste of Jesus' teaching that 'blessed are the pure in heart, for they shall see God' (Matt. 5:8). What a glorious way to lift your downtrodden heart in the midst of this life's burdens—to realise that you 'have a friend in Jesus, who will all your sorrows share,' and to gain a glimpse of eternity through the One who will always protect you with his steadfast love.

> I have a Friend whose faithful love
> Is more than all the world to me;
> 'Tis higher than the heights above,
> And deeper than the soundless sea;
> So old, so new, so strong, so true;
> Before the earth received its frame,
> He loved me—blessèd be His name!
>
> Long as I live my song shall tell
> The wonders of His matchless love:
> And when at last I rise to dwell
> In that bright home prepared above,
> My joy shall be His face to see,
> And bowing then with loud acclaim,
> I'll praise him—blessèd be His name![5]

REFLECT ON THESE POINTS:

- David is saying: God has kept his promises in the past, God is unchanging, so he will keep them again now.
- What a glorious way to lift your downtrodden heart in the midst of this life's burdens—to realise that you 'have a friend in Jesus, who will all your sorrows share,' and to gain a glimpse of eternity through the One who will always protect you with his steadfast love.

PSALM 18

In God my Saviour shall my heart rejoice

Like a number of the psalms thus far, we don't quite know exactly when this one was written. Verse 1 tells us that David '*spoke* to the LORD the words of this song on the day when the LORD delivered him from the hand of all his enemies and from the hand of Saul.' That suggests that it could have been written earlier. But Psalm 18 is unusual in that it appears in an almost identical form elsewhere in Scripture—as 2 Samuel 22 which places it towards the end of David's life.

The psalm is bookended by verses that tell us why we should praise God—for who he is (vv. 1–3), for what he has done (vv. 46–50) and because he is 'worthy to be praised' (v. 3). It's so easy for us to forget these three foundational things and without them our worship too easily becomes mechanistic and self-centred. Just in the first two verses alone, David tells us of eight things that the Lord is to him—my strength, my rock, my fortress, my deliverer, my refuge, my shield, the horn of my salvation and my stronghold! And maybe the most important word in that list is 'my', for unless you can add that first person pronoun the list becomes merely a list of facts rather than a relationship of faith.

Then in verses 4–19, David tells us of the God of deliverance. First, when David 'cried for help . . . [God] heard my voice' (v. 6). And what a contrast that is with David's godless enemies of whom we read in verse 41, 'They cried for help, but there was none to save; they cried to the LORD, but he did not answer them.' Second, David tells us that God 'rescued me from my strong enemy' (v. 17). And as one begins to be able to look back on one's life, see if you can't attest to the truth of God's merciful deliverance—not only from a life of sin, but from foolish mistakes from which God graciously rescued you. I know that's true for me!Before we move on, you might be wondering when the earth-shattering events of verses 7–15 occurred in David's life—earthquakes, hailstones, coals of fire and the like? In comparison, David's life was pretty humdrum. Alec Motyer offers an insightful answer when he describes these verses as if we're 'behind the scenes with God.'[1] He takes us back to Judges 4 and 5 where the historical account of Barak's victory over Sisera—'the LORD routed Sisera . . . by the edge of the sword' (Jdgs. 4:15)—is followed by a very different take in Deborah and Barak's song in Judges 5. As Motyer reminds us: 'On earth the battle has to be planned and forces assembled . . . yet it is only the Lord who gives the victory, and to this cause he summons all the heavenly forces at his command.'[2]

Returning to Psalm 18:20–30, David tells us of the path of holiness and that picks up the theme of Psalm 15. You can see the change of focus by simply looking at the first word of many of the verses. Verses 16, 17 and 19 all began with 'He' referring to God. But in verses 20–24 the first-person pronouns I, me or my appear fourteen times! Once more, there are echoes of Psalm 15—of 'he who walks blamelessly' (Ps. 15:2). And as we said then, when David talks of 'my righteousness' (vv. 20, 24), 'the cleanness of my hands' (v. 21) and 'I was blameless before him' (v. 23), he is not claiming sinless perfection. He knows we know better. What we're meant to see here is a general principle that 'when we live for God and try to go in his way, he cares for us and blesses us.'[3] As another commentator puts it: 'God delights to reward obedience.'[4]

'God delights to reward obedience.'

Then in verses 31–45, David tells us of the God of victories. In many ways, David is returning to his theme in verses 4–19. And he begins by reminding himself—and us—of the character of this God of victories.

> For who is God, but the LORD?
> And who is a rock, except our God? (v. 31)

But rather than telling us of the victories as the narrator as he did earlier—God did this, God did that—from verse 35 David is, as it were, in conversation with God himself.

'You have given me the shield of your salvation . . . You equipped me with strength for the battle . . . You made my enemies turn their backs to me . . . You delivered me from strife with the people . . . You made me the head of the nations' (vv. 35–43). It's a wonderful way of spending some of your daily time in prayer to remind yourself of God's character and attributes, and the psalms are a wonderful songbook to use.

The psalms are a wonderful songbook to use.

David ends with the other bookend—verses 46–50— in which he extols and worships 'my rock . . . the God of my salvation' (v. 46). 'For this,' he sings, 'I will praise you, O LORD, among the nations, and sing to your name' (v. 49). So David's great song, Psalm 18, stands in a line with the great songs of Scripture. There are the two we heard echoed in Psalm 17—Moses' song in Exodus 15 after God has delivered his people from slavery in Egypt, and his song in Deuteronomy 32 as God's people stand on the border of the Promised Land. Then there's Hannah's song (1 Samuel 2:1–10) which provides a forward-looking summary of what God was about to do—the birth of Samuel, the prophet whom God would call to anoint David as King over his people. And these all point forward to yet another song—of Mary (Lk. 1:46–55)—that we know as the Magnificat, upon the announcement to her of the imminent birth of God's Messiah. And all five songs have this in common, that Moses, Hannah, David and Mary all want to tell us about God's 'salvation' or 'Saviour'.[5]

So what do these words mean to those who lived before the death of Christ? Salvation in the Old Testament is used in two ways. It can mean the deliverance God brings his people from disease, trouble or enemies. He saved them from Egypt and later from Babylon. But the rescue from Egypt—the exodus—also pointed forward to a full and final saving of his people in a spiritual sense. David, like all those who lived in Old Testament times, was saved in the spiritual sense 'in the same way in which a person is saved today—by grace through faith in a redeemer who was to come, just as today a person is saved by grace through faith in the redeemer who has already come.'[6] They looked forward to Christ; we look back. The Old Testament sacrifices pointed forward to Christ. So Moses and Hannah and David, and of course Mary, are in this sense looking forward to God's fulfilment of his promise of a Saviour that he made to Adam and Eve (Gen. 3:15), to Abraham (Gen. 12:1–3) and to David (2 Sam. 7:12–16). So when David in Psalm 18:46 sings: 'The LORD lives, and blessed be my rock, and exalted be the God of my salvation' he might easily have continued, as may we:

> Tell out, my soul, the greatness of the Lord!
> Unnumbered blessings give my spirit voice;

Tender to me the promise of His word;
In God my Saviour shall my heart rejoice.

Tell out, my soul, the greatness of His name!
Make known His might, the deeds His arm has
    done;
His mercy sure, from age to age the same;
His holy name—the Lord, the Mighty One.[7]

REFLECT ON THESE POINTS:

- As one looks back on one's life, see if you can't attest to the truth of God's merciful deliverance— not only from a life of sin, but from foolish mistakes from which God graciously rescued you.
- What we're meant to see here is a general principle that 'when we live for God and try to go in his way, he cares for us and blesses us.' (James Boice)

PSALM 19

Lord, be Thy Word my rule

For the British theologian C.S. Lewis (1898–1963), Psalm 19 was 'the greatest poem in the Psalter and one of the greatest lyrics in the world.'[1] Here is a psalm that has inspired many a majestic musical setting. It's inspired two great hymns—Joseph Addison's 'The Spacious Firmament on High' (1712) and Isaac Watts' 'The Heavens Declare Thy Glory, Lord (1719)—as well as the most famous chorus in Joseph Haydn's 'The Creation' (1799), 'The Heavens Are Telling the Glory of God.' It's a psalm about God's revelation of himself to humankind— through creation (vv. 1–6) and through the Scriptures (vv. 7–11). You need to see that 'revelation' link in order to make sense of what otherwise appears to be the *non sequitur* of verse 7. John Stott sees the psalm as showing three revelations: a general revelation (vv. 1–6); a special revelation (vv. 7–10); a personal revelation (vv. 11–14).[2] For Michael Wilcock, there are three voices—the heavens, the law and the psalmist.[3] To Derek Kidner, this psalm is about 'the Skies and the Scriptures.'[4]

The opening verse brings us an echo of Psalm 8:3 where David sang to God of the heavens being 'the work of your fingers, the moon and the stars, which you have set in place.' The Old Testament scholar E.J. Young writes: 'The entirety of creation speaks with voices clear and positive of the glory of the Holy God. Wherever we turn our eyes, we see the marks of His majesty, and should lift our hearts in praise to Him who is holy.'[5] And God's general revelation in creation is a theme of which the apostle Paul speaks in both his preaching and writing.[6] Such revelation leaves mankind 'without excuse' (Rom. 1:20) as to God's existence and creative power. This revelation is continuous—'day after day . . . night after night' (v. 2, NIV)—as well as being abundant in that it 'pours forth' (v. 2, NIV) in wordless speech (v. 3); a glorious paradox. How true that 'night to night reveals knowledge' (v. 2) for until comparatively recently, without the night skies we would have presumed that we inhabited an empty universe. Joseph Addison captures the sermon preached by the sky at night when he writes that the sparkling constellations are:

> For ever singing as they shine,
> 'The hand that made us is divine.'[7]

Then in verses 4b–6, David uses the sun as the prime exhibit showing off God's creation, using some mixed metaphors of both a bridegroom and a running athlete (vv. 5–6). In his paraphrase, Isaac Watts takes this picture and relates it to Christ and the gospel:

> Nor shall Thy spreading gospel rest
> Till through the world Thy truth has run;

> Till Christ has all the nations blest,
> That see the light or feel the sun.[8]

He also then creates an ingenious link to take us from God's general revelation in creation to his special revelation in his Word:

> Great Sun of righteousness, arise;
> Bless the dark world with heavenly light;
> Thy gospel makes the simple wise,
> Thy laws are pure, Thy judgements right.

And it's a biblical link too, for the apostle Paul makes the same link when in Romans 10 he quotes Psalm 19:4 to show that the message of God's salvation has been shown to all. 'Have they not heard?' asks Paul. 'Indeed they have, for "Their sound has gone out to all the earth, and their words to the ends of the world"' (Rom. 10:18).

Verses 7–9 give us an example of parallelism in Hebrew poetry as the law,[9] the testimony, the precepts, the commandment, the fear and the rules (or decrees) of the Lord are introduced, and we're told for each what it is and what it does. God's Word is, David tells us, perfect, sure, right, pure, clean, true and righteous. And it revives the soul, makes the simple wise, rejoices the heart, enlightens the eyes and endures for ever. One could preach a sermon on those verses alone! But it poses the question: Is that how you regard God's Word, the Bible? Is it daily, through God's Holy Spirit, doing those things in your heart and life? Sometimes preachers try to help us by telling us that the Bible is 'God's instruction manual.' I know what they mean, but who reads instruction manuals? And daily? The Puritan Thomas Watson (c. 1620–1686) had better advice. 'Read the Scriptures,' he wrote, 'not only as history but as a love letter sent to you from God which may affect your heart.'[10] David also tells us how precious the Scriptures are to him—'More to be desired are they than gold, even much fine gold' (v. 10). We saw in our study of Psalm 12 how the Bible has been described as 'the most valuable thing this world affords.' Is that how you regard it?

And then the psalm transitions into the final section, a personal revelation of God to each Bible-obeying believer. Essentially what David tells us is that the Bible should do two things for you—it reveals sin (vv. 12–13) and promotes holiness (v. 14). God's Word acts as a mirror. A mirror tells us two things: it explicitly tells us what we are like, and it implicitly tells us what we then ought to do about it. Paul writes of how 'through the law comes knowledge of sin' (Rom. 3:20). David knows that too which is why he prays to be kept from 'presumptuous [that is, wilful] sins' and asks that 'they may not have dominion over me' (v. 13). That's, if you will, the negative. But David

> **The Bible should do two things for you— it reveals sin and promotes holiness.**

123

also prays positively, that 'the words of my mouth and the meditation of my heart be acceptable' in God's sight (v. 14). It's a wonderful prayer to make your very own.

He ends by talking of God as his redeemer. Redemption is a word that should be most dear to every Christian. Paul writes of our 'Saviour Jesus Christ who gave himself for us to *redeem* us from all lawlessness and to purify for himself a people of his own possession who are zealous for good works' (Tit. 2:13–14). And the important point we need to see—both in that verse from Titus and here in Psalm 19—is that Christ redeems us *from* sin, but also *to* a life of holiness that is pleasing to God. That's what David is praying for in verse 14— words and thoughts that are 'acceptable' ('pleasing', NIV) in God's sight. Now there's a challenge! Some of what I think and say isn't even acceptable to me, or to my wife, let alone to God!

One small nugget which we missed. In verse 11, David tells us that in keeping of God's Word 'there is great reward.' So what is this 'reward'? Many commentators seem baffled by this and so hurriedly move on to the next verse! The reward is God himself!

> Lord, be Thy Word my rule,
> In it may I rejoice;
> Thy glory be my aim,
> Thy holy will my choice.

Thy promises my hope,
Thy providence my guard,
Thine arm my strong support,
Thyself my great reward![11]

REFLECT ON THESE POINTS:

- 'Wherever we turn our eyes, we see the marks of His majesty, and should lift our hearts in praise to Him who is holy.' (Edward Young)
- 'Read the Scriptures, not only as history but as a love letter sent to you from God which may affect your heart.' (Thomas Watson)

PSALM 20

In Thy name we go

When I lived in Godalming in Surrey, a summer's day would often tempt me to a lovely circular walk through Shackleford and over Puttenham Common. The homeward leg brought me through Puttenham village and past the local inn—The Good Intent. The pub sign shows a knight kneeling at the opening of his tent praying before battle—'The Good in Tent!' It often brought a smile to my face and thoughts of Agincourt before which, in Shakespeare's play, Henry prays:

> O God of battles! steel my soldiers' hearts;
> Possess them not with fear; take from them now
> The sense of reckoning, if the opposed numbers
> Pluck their hearts from them.
> (*Henry V*, Act IV, Scene 1)

The 9,000 English were vastly outnumbered facing some 60,000 Frenchmen. But Henry was resolute and when the Earl of Westmorland apparently suggested Henry could do with reinforcements, the King replied: 'I would not have a single man more. If God gives us the victory, it will be plain we owe it to His grace.'[1]

You're probably wondering what the connection is

between the Battle of Agincourt and Psalm 20. Well, Psalms 20 and 21 come as a pair of what we call royal psalms because they're about 'the king.' Psalm 20 ends, 'O LORD, save the king!' and Psalm 21 begins, 'O LORD, in your strength the king rejoices' and most commentators agree that both relate to a time of war—Psalm 20 on the eve of battle, and Psalm 21 following victory. We're not told which battle these psalms relate to, nor which foreign powers were attacking Israel. David was certainly in the habit of seeking God's assistance before a military campaign.[2] But if you want to get a flavour of this kind of setting then read the account of Asa preparing for battle in 2 Chronicles 14, or of Jehoshaphat against the Moabites and others in 2 Chronicles 20. It's good to have godly leaders who turn to God in prayer at such times.

As well as being a royal psalm, Psalm 20 is also a liturgical psalm in which the 'congregation' play an important part. Indeed, it is they who are speaking in verses 1–5 in what is really a prayer to God for their king, although it's addressed to God via the king who is the 'you' (singular). And in the first four verses they make eight requests to God for the king: that God would answer, protect, help, support, remember and favour him, and that he would 'grant you your heart's desire and fulfil all your plans.' The most eye-catching petition comes in verse 1: 'May the name of the God of Jacob protect you!' In the Bible names are important, especially the names

127

of God. Indeed, knowing God's names is critical to our understanding of God himself. As Derek Kidner writes: 'The divine name was a token of God's self-revelation' to his people.[3] That's why God's name was—and still should be—held in such high regard. 'Hallowed be your *name*,' Jesus bids his disciples pray (Matt. 6:9). And in one of the most famous pre-battle prayers, King Asa prays, 'For we rest on You, and in Your *name* we go against this multitude' (2 Chron. 14:11, NKJV).

And 'the God of Jacob' reminds us that ours is a covenant-making, promise-keeping God.[4] In verse 5 we see how that the people's fate is tied to the fate of the king. They want to be able to 'shout for joy' when God gives the king victory.

'The God of Jacob' reminds us that ours is a covenant-making, promise-keeping God.

Now in verse 6, the king speaks. Commentators are divided as to whether he speaks just verse 6 with the people chiming in again with verses 7 and 8, or whether the king speaks the whole of this stanza, verses 6–8. Given the way the stanzas fall, the latter seems most likely. If that be so, the king has three things to say. First, in verse 6, he reassures his people that God does answer prayer. Second—and this is maybe the big takeaway of this psalm—he wants to challenge them about who, or what, it is in which they place their trust.

Some trust in chariots and some in horses,
but we trust in the name of the LORD our God. (v. 7)

God had already addressed his people on the subject of chariots and horses through Moses. In Deuteronomy 20:1 he told them not to fear them. The trouble with chariots and horses is that they don't always perform as expected, especially when God takes a hand. Remember the events at the Red Sea? Pharaoh's army was pursuing the Israelites who, with divine intervention, had just crossed the Red Sea 'on dry ground.' The Egyptian army follow, but: 'In the morning watch the LORD threw the Egyptian forces into a panic, clogging their chariot wheels' (Ex. 14:24–25). The rest, as they say, is history. The application for us is surely quite clear. Who or what is it that you are trusting in? I'm writing this in the midst of the Covid-19 pandemic during which so many things that appeared trustworthy—jobs, investments, health to name but three—have proved to be anything but trustworthy. When he was Chancellor of the Exchequer, Nigel (now Lord) Lawson said that the National Health Service is 'the nearest thing the British people have to a religion.'[5] Scripture is clear: 'Trust in the LORD with all your heart' (Prov. 3:5).

First the king reassures, second he challenges, third (v. 8) he warns. 'They,' he says—those who are trusting in the chariots and horses or their modern-day equivalents—'collapse and fall.' Remember how Psalm 1 ended? 'But the way of the wicked will perish' (v. 6). It's a grim warning. And to encourage us to choose the right path, he adds, 'but we'—those who put their whole trust in God—'rise and stand upright.' And reading that promise with Christian eyes, those who have trusted in Christ will truly 'rise and stand upright.'

> For the Lord himself will descend from heaven with a cry of command, with the voice of an archangel, and with the sound of the trumpet of God. And the dead in Christ will rise first (1 Thess. 4:16).

So what to take away from Psalm 20? Three things. First, the challenge from verse 7 about where our trust really is. Second, to pray for our leaders—kings, queens, presidents, prime ministers, or whoever God has in his sovereign will placed over us. No, they are not in the same anointed position over God's people as was King David, but we are bidden by Scripture to pray 'for kings and all who are in high positions, that we may lead a peaceful and quiet life, godly and dignified in every way' (1 Tim. 2:2). Third, we need to see what human kings were unable to accomplish—even David—Jesus brought to fruition. As one commentator puts it: 'What the kings represented at their best, Christ epitomised in his life and work and will fulfil at the Second Coming as victorious Lord.'[6] What David achieved as a 'man after God's own heart' was frittered away by his mostly ungodly descendants. What Christ achieved, like his Word, 'lives and abides forever' (1 Peter 1:23, NKJV).

> We go in faith, our own great weakness feeling,
> And needing more each day Thy grace to know;
> Yet from our hearts, a song of triumph pealing:
> 'We rest on Thee, and in Thy name we go.'[7]

REFLECT ON THESE POINTS:

- In the Bible names are important, especially the names of God. Indeed, knowing God's names is critical to our understanding of God himself.
- The psalmist wants to challenge us about who, or what, it is in which we place our trust.
- What David achieved as a 'man after God's own heart' was frittered away by his mostly ungodly descendants. What Christ achieved 'lives and abides forever.'

Psalm 21

Our cheerful songs

You doubtless remember the story that Luke relates of the ten lepers that Jesus healed, telling them to show themselves to the priests which was what the Old Testament law required. But you'll remember, the story doesn't end there.

> And as they went they were cleansed. Then one of them, when he saw that he was healed, turned back, praising God with a loud voice; and he fell on his face at Jesus' feet, giving him thanks. Now he was a Samaritan. Then Jesus answered, 'Were not ten cleansed? Where are the nine? Was no one found to return and give praise to God except this foreigner?' (Lk. 17:14–18).

Psalms 20 and 21 are very much a pair. We saw in the last exposition that it seemed likely that Psalm 20 was set on the eve of one of King David's great battles. It concluded with the people praying: 'O LORD, save the king! May he answer us when we call' (Ps. 20:9). It is therefore highly likely that Psalm 21 was sung just after God had indeed given them the victory. In the opening words, the people sing: 'O LORD, in your strength the king rejoices and in your salvation how greatly he exults' (Ps. 21:1). In Psalm 20, the people had prayed that God would give the king 'your heart's desire and fulfil all your plans' (Ps. 20:4). In Psalm 21, they praise God, for 'You have given [the king] his heart's desire and have not withheld the request of his lips' (Ps. 21:2). Psalm 20 is the prayer; Psalm 21 is the praise.

All this raises an important question: How careful, how eager are you to give thanks to Almighty God when he answers *your* 'heart's desire'? Are you the one who returns? Are you singing Psalm 21 after praying Psalm 20? In the previous exposition, I likened David's situation before the battle to that of Henry V's prayer before Agincourt. Whilst I'm not putting the English king on a par with the king after God's own heart, Henry was quick to follow David's example and give thanks to God. With victory achieved, but only a few of his men killed, Shakespeare has Henry tell his commanders:

> O God, thy arm was here;
> And not to us, but to thy arm alone,
> Ascribe we all! . . . Take it, God,
> For it is none but thine! (*Henry V*, Act IV, Scene 8)

Henry then orders that they will sing Psalm 115—'Not to us, O LORD, not to us, but to your name give glory'—followed by the *Te Deum*, the Canticle which begins:

> We praise Thee, O God: we acknowledge Thee

to be the Lord.
All the earth doth worship Thee, the Father
everlasting!

Back at Psalm 21, we can say that it falls into two main parts: a thanksgiving for past victories (vv. 1–6) and a thanksgiving for future victories (vv. 8–12)—verses 7 and 13 standing somewhat on their own as we shall see. In the opening stanza, the people give thanks to God, naming six blessings that he has granted to the king, one in each verse. In verse 1, the word rendered 'salvation' (ESV) or 'victories' (NIV) is one which denotes deliverance from a dangerous situation. It's the word used by Joab when he tells his brother Abishai that 'if the Ammonites are too strong for you, then I will come to *rescue* you' (2 Sam. 10:11, NIV). So this is salvation in a temporal rather than a spiritual sense. In the following verses, they give thanks to God for answered prayer (v. 2), the blessings of victory (v. 3), long life (v. 4), glory, splendour and majesty (v. 5), and for joy and gladness in God's presence (v. 6).

The singers here in Psalm 21 are rejoicing at the blessings that God has given to them through their king. Surely that ought to set the tongue of the Christian singing as you and I remember the blessings that God has given, gives and will give us through our King, the Lord Jesus Christ. And if you need a reminder, then read Paul's stirring opening to his letter to the Ephesians:

> Blessed be the God and Father of our Lord Jesus Christ, who has blessed us in Christ with every spiritual blessing in the heavenly places, even as he chose us in him before the foundation of the world, that we should be holy and blameless before him (Eph. 1:3–4).

Hebrew poetry often puts the main point in the middle rather than at the end, and Psalm 21 is an example. Verse 7—the middle verse—is the transitional verse between the two main stanzas, and it also contains that great doctrine of God's 'steadfast love' (*hesed*) that we've seen in earlier psalms. 'For the king trusts in the LORD, and through the steadfast love of the Most High he shall not be moved.' Here we have the two sides of the covenant: 'trust', which is our part; 'steadfast love', which is God's part. As Dale Ralph Davis comments on this verse, God's '*Hesed*-love is not simply love, it's love with super-glue on it!'[1]

In verses 8–12, the psalmist looks forward to the victories that God will yet win over his enemies—the 'You' and 'Your' in these verses. Some readers might think that the psalm might be much improved had it ended at verse 7! After all, this 'blazing oven', 'swallow them up',

Hebrew poetry often puts the main point in the middle rather than at the end.

'consuming fire' (v. 9) and destruction (v. 10) doesn't sound very attractive. It's not meant to. And in case you're taken in by the 'Oh, don't worry, this is just the way folk used to talk in the *Old* Testament, so we don't have to worry any more' argument, then dip into Jesus' teaching in Luke 25:31–46 and note the warning of the writer to the Hebrews that 'It is a fearful thing to fall into the hands of the living God' (Heb. 10:31).

Like its predecessor, Psalm 21 has a final verse in which the people join to sign off with a collective voice: 'Be exalted, O LORD, in your strength! We will sing and praise your power' (v. 13). The last line is invitational in its tone—'Let us sing, let us praise your power.' The thankful remembrance of God's mercies should lead us to such a response. But before we can be thankful, we must remember. In 1897, Rudyard Kipling was asked to write a poem celebrating sixty years of the reign of Queen Victoria. Everyone expected a poem singing the praises of Great Britain and her Queen. What Kipling wrote was a warning:

> Lord God of hosts, be with us yet,
> Lest we forget, lest we forget.[2]

Lest we forget! Take time to think of all God's many mercies to you and let that tune your heart to respond to the psalmist's final invitation, 'Come, let us sing and praise Your power.'

Come, let us join our cheerful songs
With angels round the throne;
Ten thousand thousand are their tongues,
But all their joys are one.

'Worthy the Lamb that died,' they cry,
'To be exalted thus!'
'Worthy the Lamb,' our lips reply,
'For He was slain for us.'[3]

REFLECT ON THESE POINTS:

- How careful, how eager are you to give thanks to Almighty God when he answers your 'heart's desire'?
- God's 'Hesed-love is not simply love, it's love with super-glue on it!' (Dale Ralph Davis)

PSALM 22

It is finished!

One of the benefits of reading the psalms consecutively is that we appreciate the wonderful changes in mood from one psalm to another. Here two psalms about the king triumphing over his enemies with military might are now followed by a psalm about a king who suffers. And that brings us to address the thorny issue of who is being referred to in Psalm 22. Who is the 'me' of verse 1? As usual, John Stott is helpful when he states that at one level: 'the narrative of his afflictions is so vivid in its detail that it undoubtedly depicts a true and literal experience.'[1] But at another level: 'Christian eyes cannot read this psalm, nor Christian lips sing it, without applying it to the sufferings of Christ and his subsequent glory.'[2] We need to read and apply it at both levels. We can do no better than to interpret Scripture through Scripture and so as the apostle Peter says of another psalm, 'Being therefore a prophet ... [David] foresaw and spoke of ... the Christ' (Acts 2:30–31). We first consider the psalm in its Old Testament context.

Psalm 22 is made up of two unequal and contrasting halves. The first half, verses 1–21, represent what John Stott calls the cry of anguish. First, there is David's cry of forsakenness to God (vv. 1–2). 'My God, my God, why have you forsaken me?' What is extraordinary is that more than all the mockery and the pain and agony that follows in the following verses, it is David's sense of God-forsakenness that is his greatest cause of suffering. 'This is not the "why" of impatience or despair, not the sinful questioning of one whose heart rebels against his chastening, but rather the cry of a lost child who cannot understand why his father has left him, and longs to see his father's face again. It is the question of faith as well as of an anguish that cannot be told.'[3] We know this because despite the questions, God is still 'my God'—not once, not twice, but three times in these opening two verses.

How wonderful the psalms are at giving voice to even our most raw emotions—of suffering, bereavement, loneliness, physical pain. Some say that Christians shouldn't ask such questions, shouldn't feel God-forsaken. But Bishop Ryle wrote of how the true Christian 'though chosen and beloved of the Father, may sometimes feel God's face turned away from them. They too, sometimes from illness of body, sometimes from peculiar affliction, sometimes from carelessness of walk, sometimes from God's will to draw them nearer to Himself, may be constrained to cry' these same words.[4]

After David's cry come David's troubles (vv. 12–18). These fall into two types: the evil men who surround him like bulls, a roaring lion or a pack of wild dogs (vv. 12–13,

16–18); and his sickness that brings him close to death (vv. 14–15). How much of our distress is caused either by those who make our life unpleasant or by the frailty of our own bodies?

But even in the anguish, there are glimpses of hope—introduced by the words 'yet' (vv. 3 and 9) or 'but' (v. 19). David takes heart from God's past mercies to his ancestors.

> They trusted and you delivered them.
> To you they cried and were rescued;
> in you they trusted and were not put to shame.
> (vv. 4–5)

He takes heart from God's past mercies to him—God's guarding of him through birth and childhood (vv. 9–11). Looking back thankfully is a great tonic for the downhearted Christian. And so is prayer, to which David resorts in verses 19–21—come, deliver, save, he prays.

Looking back thankfully is a great tonic for the downhearted Christian.

Then as verse 22 begins, David switches from the minor to the major key as the voice of 'praise' is on his lips—the word comes four times in the next five verses. We're not told how the deliverance came, simply that God 'has heard, when he cried to him' (v. 24). And now he wants everyone else to join him in worshipful praise. As John Stott puts it, 'The true worshipper is always thus missionary-minded: he cannot conceive of praising God alone.'[5] David will praise God both 'in the great congregation' (v. 23), that is with his fellow Israelites, and with 'all the families of the nations' (v. 27) as David prophetically looks ahead to the conversion of the Gentiles.

And that brings us back to the One of whom this psalm also speaks so clearly, for it would be Christ who would come both as 'a light for revelation to the Gentiles, and for glory to [God's] people Israel' (Lk. 2:32). And this is His psalm too, as well as David's. Jesus quotes verse 1 from the cross (Matt. 27:26, Mark 15:34). The mocking of verse 7 is fulfilled by the Jewish rulers (Lk. 23:35), the Roman soldiers (Lk. 23:36–37) and by one of the criminals crucified with Jesus (Lk. 23:39). Verse 8 is spoken almost word for word by the chief priests, scribes and elders (Matt. 27:43). Verses 14–17 describe death by crucifixion centuries before such a barbaric form of execution was even used. And all four gospel writers record the fulfilment of David's prophecy in verse 18 when the Roman soldiers cast lots for Jesus' seamless tunic (Matt. 27:35, Mk. 15:24, Lk. 23:34, Jn. 19:24). Thus the psalm 'looks forward to Christ. It is a foreshadowing of Him and His passion.'[6]

And it's not only the first half of the psalm that finds prophetic fulfilment in Christ. As the psalm closes talking of how 'all the ends of the earth shall remember and turn to the LORD, and all the families of the nations shall worship before you' (v. 27) our Christian eyes glance ahead to Jesus' great commission, to Pentecost and beyond to the worldwide church. The psalm's final verse says: 'They shall come and proclaim his righteousness to a people yet unborn, that he has done it.' And the 'it' is the salvation of our souls that Christ won at Calvary. He has, indeed, done it. For as he proclaimed in his final words from the cross, 'It is finished!' (Jn. 19:30).

> Hark! the voice of love and mercy
> Sounds aloud from Calvary;
> See, it rends the rocks asunder,
> Shakes the earth, and veils the sky:
> 'It is finished! It is finished!'
> Hear the dying Saviour cry.
>
> 'It is finished!' O what pleasure
> Do the wondrous words afford!
> Heavenly blessings without measure
> Flow to us from Christ the Lord:
> 'It is finished! It is finished!'
> Saints the dying words record.[7]

REFLECT ON THESE POINTS:

- The true Christian, 'though chosen and beloved of the Father, may sometimes feel God's face turned away from them. They too, sometimes from illness of body, sometimes from peculiar affliction, sometimes from carelessness of walk, sometimes from God's will to draw them nearer to Himself, may be constrained to cry' these same words. (Bishop Ryle)

- The psalm 'looks forward to Christ. It is a foreshadowing of Him and His passion.' (Bishop Perowne)

PSALM 23

Thy goodness faileth never

It is probably true to say that no six consecutive verses of Scripture are more often read, or committed to memory, or sung in the form of a hymn, than those of Psalm 23. Furthermore, it is a psalm that takes us seamlessly from God the Father to God the Son. For the shepherd of whom David writes is both. Just as the preceding psalm told us of the Good Shepherd who lays down his life for the sheep (Jn. 10:11), so this psalm tells us how the Good Shepherd knows his sheep and they know him (Jn. 10:14). Bishop Robert Lowth (1710–87) asked: 'What can be conceived sweeter or finer than this representation of God as a Shepherd?'[1]

And Psalm 23 is really about God himself. He's introduced in the opening words as 'the Lord', the great personal name for God, first disclosed to Moses at the burning bush—the 'I Am Who I Am,' the covenant-keeping God. Thus far in the Psalter, God has been spoken of using various metaphors—a king, a righteous judge, a shield, a rock, a stronghold[2]—but all of these are either distant or impersonal. How wonderful to read of God as shepherd. Shepherding was regarded as lowly work, nourishing, guiding and protecting the sheep. But Jesus himself took the metaphor for his own in the parable of the lost sheep (Lk. 15:1–7) and of his being the Good Shepherd (Jn. 10:1–18). And God is not just a shepherd but to David he is *my* shepherd. And only if you can truly say that first part of the verse can you claim the second half—'I shall not want.' The focus here is not on 'wanting' but on 'not lacking' something you need. Now in the remainder of the psalm, David tells us of the life to which every true believer can look forward with God as your Good Shepherd.

First, God provides an abundant life with spiritual food and rest (v. 2). Henry Blunt sees the 'green pastures' and the 'still waters' as God's provision of things such as the Lord's Day, the Scriptures, the Lord's Supper and prayer which nourish the soul.[3] One might have expected David to start with things for us to do. But we begin, the psalm teaches, by resting in him who has done everything for us. 'Come to me, all who labour and are heavy laden, and I will give you rest,' promises the Good Shepherd (Matt. 11:28). Are you resting in Christ, enjoying all that he has done for you and provides daily for you?

As part of the believer's abundant life, God also provides forgiveness and guidance (v. 3). 'He restores my soul,' says the psalmist, from repented and pardoned sin. And David knew this from experience. After he repented of his great sin with Bathsheba, God sent the prophet Nathan to tell David, 'The LORD has put away your sin' (2 Sam. 12:13). And he says the same to you when you, likewise, repent in penitence and faith, and your soul is restored. What's more, he will 'lead you in the paths of righteousness'—literally, 'the right paths'—the ones that take you to your desired and eternal haven. Henry Blunt writes:

> How glorious it will be to look back through the long course of our heavenly Father's merciful dealings and see the now hidden hand which is directing and arranging all—our trials, our sorrows, our sicknesses, our distresses—all sanctified to us by His Holy Spirit, all forming part of the wondrous plan, leading us through the green pastures, placing us beside the still waters, and laying us at the foot of the cross whence alone we can be carried from earth to heaven.[4]

Second, God provides a secure life even as you 'walk through the valley of the shadow of death' (v. 4). If you've visited the Bible lands, you will know that green pastures and still waters are something of a rarity. Much more common are the deep, dark and usually waterless wadis in which the oppressive heat makes this dangerous and fearful terrain for sheep and for humans. But even here, the shepherd makes ample provision. He has a rod—a short mace-like implement for defending his sheep against wild animals. He has a staff—like a walking stick with which to nudge and guide the sheep as they traverse this dangerous route. And to countless generations of believers, these words have brought comfort as their moment of death has approached. For even death itself has become in Christ no more than 'a shadow.' Matthew Henry writes: 'There is no substantial evil in it; the shadow of a serpent will not sting nor the shadow of a sword kill.'[5]

Third, God provides a blessed life (v. 5). Here David changes the image to one of greater intimacy. God changes from shepherd to host and David changes from sheep to honoured table guest. In Old Testament times, to eat and drink at someone's table created a bond of mutual loyalty. And oil and wine in the Bible speak of holiness and joy. In Psalm 104 we read of God giving 'wine to gladden the heart of man, oil to make his face shine and bread to strengthen man's heart' (Ps. 104:15). Here we have a picture of communion with God himself. Yet we see that even in this abundant, secure and blessed life, all is still played out 'in the presence of my enemies.' They don't disappear; they just lose their ultimate significance.

To be God's honoured table guest is not just calling by for one meal.

But there is still more! For in the final verse we discover that to be God's honoured table guest is not just calling by for one meal.

In verse 6, we discover that we are not just table guests, not just house guests, but that we 'dwell in the house of the LORD, forever.' Thus through abundant life, secure life

147

and blessed life, God leads us to eternal life—'life in all its fullness' (Jn. 10:10, GNT). We shall hear more of this theme of dwelling in God's house later in the Psalter most notably in Psalm 84. In its immediate context it spoke of taking refuge in the Temple, but we read it in the light of Jesus telling us that, 'In my Father's house are many rooms . . . And if I go and prepare a place for you, I will come again and take you to myself, that where I am you may be also' (Jn. 14:2–3).

But you don't have to wait until eternity to enjoy God's presence. Indeed, if you desire to dwell with God in eternity, you should be increasingly anxious to enjoy him now. Remember that his sheep hear his voice, and follow him—now. And all the more so as you approach those years of your life when failing faculties whisper that soon you will be walking through that shadowy valley of death. Pull away from those things that draw your heart away from God and spend more time in prayer, in reading, studying and meditation of the Scriptures, spending time when you can with Christian brothers and sisters. So that when that hour arrives, as it inevitably will, you will be enabled to say with the apostle, 'I have fought a good fight, I have finished the race, I have kept the faith. Henceforth there is laid up for me the crown of righteousness which the Lord, the righteous judge, will award to me on that Day, and not only to me but also to all who have loved his appearing' (2 Tim. 4:7–8). 'And I shall dwell in the house of the LORD forever.'

> And so through all the length of days
> Thy goodness faileth never:
> Good Shepherd, may I sing Thy praise
> Within Thy house for ever.[6]

REFLECT ON THESE POINTS:

- 'What can be conceived sweeter or finer than this representation of God as a Shepherd?' (Robert Lowth).
- 'How glorious it will be to look back through the long course of our heavenly Father's merciful dealings and see the now hidden hand which is directing and arranging all—our trials, our sorrows, our sicknesses, our distresses—all sanctified to us by His Holy Spirit.' (Henry Blunt)

PSALM 24

Lift up your heads

Most commentaries suggest that this psalm might have been written to celebrate the arrival of the Ark of the Covenant into Jerusalem as recorded in 2 Samuel 6. To Israel, the ark represented God himself and that would fit with the cry in verses 7 and 9 for the city's gates and doors to be 'lifted up' so 'that the King of glory may come in.' It divides into three stanzas in which we see the true God, the true worshipper and the true King.

Standing between Cornhill and Threadneedle Street in the City of London, the Royal Exchange dates from the sixteenth century as the commercial centre of the city. The current building, opened by Queen Victoria in 1844, has at its west end a portico of eight Corinthian columns above which is a pediment frieze with a central figure representing Commerce. But unnoticed by the crowds that pass beneath is the biblical inscription at the centre of the frieze: 'The earth is the LORD's and the fulness thereof'—the opening line of this psalm in the King James Version. Here in the first two verses we meet the true God—the Creator and Sustainer of his universe. This is emphasised even more in the Hebrew where the opening word is 'Yahweh'—the Lord. It reads like a banner headline. The whole earth, and everything and everyone in it, belongs to God. How many folk do you hear today talking about 'our world', or 'our planet'? No! It's God's. As Charles Spurgeon elaborates: 'Men are not their own, nor may they call their substance their own: they are God's rightful servants.'[1]

From the true God, the psalmist moves to the true worshippers (vv. 3–6) with a clear echo of the first three verses of Psalm 15. Again, we can take these two questions (v. 3) on two levels: who can truly worship God, but also, who can enter God's heaven? Verse 4 contains two positives and two negatives. First, the true worshipper has 'clean hands and a pure heart.' This is what Jesus meant when he taught: 'Blessed are the pure in heart, for they shall see God' (Matt. 5:8). The 'clean hands' of which the psalmist speaks are not a plea for use of soap and water before meals. It's certainly not recommending Pilate's infamous hand-washing exercise at the trial of our Saviour (Matt. 27:24). The psalmist here is exhorting us to purity of deed as well as holiness of thought. This is what the ceremonial washing before entering the temple was meant to signify. But we know that so many took the ceremonial to be the end in itself. 'Woe to you, scribes and Pharisees, hypocrites!' said Jesus. 'For you clean the outside of the cup and the plate, but inside are full of greed and self-indulgence' (Matt. 23:25). The first negative exhorts us not to trust ('lift up his soul') in what is false—the word literally means 'vanity' or might in the contemporary context have referred to false gods. The second negative forbids deceitful talk. These are the characteristics of the true worshipper.

But then in verse 5 we further discover that these are the people who 'will receive blessing from the Lord and righteousness from the God of his salvation.' Here we have the Old Testament version of justification by faith rather than by works. David Dickson, the seventeenth century Scottish theologian wrote of these verses:

> The holy life of the true believer is not the cause of his justification before God . . . but he shall *receive* justification and eternal life, as a free gift from God, by virtue of the covenant of grace: therefore it is said here that 'he shall receive righteousness from the God of his salvation.'[2]

To 'seek God's face' is Old Testament terminology for worshipping God.

In the New Testament, Jesus tells us clearly what this blessing is when, in his discourse on the final judgement, he states: 'Then the King will say to those on his right, "Come, you who are blessed by my Father, inherit the kingdom prepared for you from the foundation of the world"' (Matt. 25:34). 'Such is the generation of those who seek him, who seek the face of the God of Jacob' (Ps. 24:6). To 'seek God's face' is Old Testament terminology for worshipping God. It's what the true worshipper does.

Thus far, the psalmist has told us of the true God and the true worshipper. Now, in the final stanza, he tells us of the true King. Here, as we have seen before, David is writing prophetically of God's promised Messiah—the King of glory. James Boice sees the fulfilment of this prophecy in the events that occurred on what we call Palm Sunday when Jesus, the King of Glory, entered Jerusalem hailed by crowds singing, 'Blessed is the King who comes in the name of the Lord!' (Lk. 19:38). Derek Kidner suggests that the prophecy may still await fulfilment at Christ's Second Coming. But most commonly, Psalm 24 is regarded as a psalm for the Ascension of our Lord. Perowne sees the psalm as 'celebrating the return of Christ as the King of Glory to His heavenly throne, and the inauguration of that dominion which He thence exercises in the world.'[3]

Christ's ascension is a much-neglected event in so many churches these days.

One must remark in passing with some sadness that Christ's ascension is a much-neglected event in so many churches these days. Each year, many faithful and evangelical churches will proclaim Jesus born, crucified, died and risen again, but make no reference at all to the climactic event of our Lord's ascension into heaven thereby neglecting to preach the theological significance of this great event. Luke writes of Christ's ascension both in his gospel (Lk. 24:51) and in his follow-up volume (Acts 1:6–11). Paul and Peter both refer to it in their letters, as does the writer to the Hebrews.[4] Peter, an eye witness of the event, writes in his first letter of Jesus 'who has gone into heaven and is at the right hand of God, with angels, authorities, and powers having been subjected to him' (1 Pet. 3:22). And the writer to the Hebrews reminds us that 'After making purification for sins, [Jesus] sat down at the right hand of the Majesty on high' (Heb. 1:4). The Ascension is therefore a sign that Christ's atoning work was complete and final. It is also a reminder that he is seated, awaiting that moment when he will return 'in the same way as [the disciples] saw him go into heaven' (Acts 1:11) to establish the kingdom of God on the earth. It is all this that is so wonderfully anticipated in these final four glorious verses of Psalm 24.

But maybe you're thinking, 'Well that's all very wonderful, but I shall never enter heaven. I don't have those clean hands and pure heart which God prescribes as essential for those who would "ascend the hill of the LORD" or "stand in his holy place".' If that is you, then look to Christ himself. He has, as it were, already climbed that hill for you and has entered heaven as your forerunner (Heb. 6:20). And, as Charles Spurgeon reminds us, he will also through his Holy Spirit 'create in you a new heart and a right spirit' for 'faith in Jesus is the work of the Holy Spirit, and has all virtues wrapped up in it.'[5] So you too can with confidence look forward to that time when these truths will be written not just on London's Royal Exchange but will, as it were, 'be written in letters of light across the sky.'[6]

> Lift up your heads, you mighty gates,
> Behold, the King of glory waits!
> The King of kings is drawing near,
> The Saviour of the world is here!
> Salvation, life he comes to bring,
> Prepare your hearts, rejoice and sing.[7]

REFLECT ON THESE POINTS:

- 'Men are not their own, nor may they call their substance their own: they are God's rightful servants.' (Charles Spurgeon)
- 'The holy life of the true believer is not the cause of his justification before God ... but he shall receive justification and eternal life, as a free gift from God, by virtue of the covenant of grace.' (David Dickson)

155

PSALM 25

Walking with Jesus

Set among hills in the midst of five valleys,
this peaceful little market town we inhabit
refuses (vociferously) to be a conformer.
Once home of the cloth it gave its name to,
uphill and down again its streets lead you.
Despite its faults, it leaves us all charmed.

This short poem by Paul Hansford extols the beauties of the Gloucestershire town of Stroud. It's obvious when it's pointed out, but the poem is an acrostic—the first letters of its six lines making the name 'Stroud'. Indeed, Hansford's poem is a double acrostic as the last letters of each of the lines also spell out the town's name! David wasn't quite that eccentric, but Psalm 25 is an acrostic—each successive verse beginning with the next letter of the twenty-two letter Hebrew alphabet, well almost. Other psalms—34 and 37 for example—follow a similar pattern. An acrostic makes learning easier, but it can mean that such psalms lack an easy to spot structure and therefore make them more of a challenge to study.

So what is the main theme of this psalm? We need to do a bit of detective work. We saw in Psalms 5 and 21 how

Hebrew poetry often reaches its climax—its main point— in the middle, and that might give us a clue here. It's possible that verse 22 was added at a later date making the original psalm one of 21 verses and verse 11 the pivotal verse: 'For your name's sake, O LORD, pardon my guilt, for it is great.' Michael Wilcock points out that there are echoes of Psalm 1 which talked of two paths—the way of the righteous and the way of the wicked. Here in Psalm 25, David clearly wants to walk in 'the way of the righteous' (Ps. 1:6) and to this end he directs his prayer to God. 'Make me to know *your ways*, O LORD; teach me *your paths*,' he prays in verse 4. He knows that God is 'good and upright . . . therefore he instructs sinners in *the way*. He leads the humble in what is right, and teaches the humble *his way*' (vv. 8–9). Again, in verse 10, he talks of how 'all *the paths of the LORD* are steadfast love and faithfulness, for those who keep his covenant and his testimonies' and in verse 12 how that the one who fears the Lord, God will 'instruct in *the way* that he should choose.'

But such phrases not only point us back to Psalm 1 but forward to the New Testament where Jesus uses the same metaphor of the spiritual life being a walk along a certain way. In his Sermon on the Mount, Jesus talks of two 'ways'—one that is wide and easy but leads to destruction, and the other that is narrow and hard but leads to life (Matt. 7:13–14). The apostle John records Jesus as telling his disciples that 'I am the way' (Jn. 14:6). And Luke records that the name 'the Way' was widely used as a title for the Christian faith in the early years of the church.[1]

So how are we going to live to ensure that we are walking in God's way, in his path? David suggests at least five things we need to be doing. First, we need to be waiting for God (v. 5). This suggests an ever-patient trusting in God alone—trusting his promises, his provision and his timing. We need to pray with William Cowper:

> Great Shepherd of Thy chosen few,
> Thy former mercies here renew;
> Here to our waiting hearts proclaim
> The sweetness of Thy saving name.[2]

Second, we need to be learning about God, allowing him to be our supreme teacher and guide (vv. 4–5). This is what's so wonderful about the Bible, but the Psalms in particular, that through it God teaches us so much about himself—his character and his attributes. In

We need to be learning about God, allowing him to be our supreme teacher and guide.

this psalm alone, God is revealed to us as faithful (v. 3), merciful (v. 6), good and upright (v. 8) and gracious (v. 16), as well as being our Saviour (v. 5), our friend (v. 14), our deliverer and refuge (v. 20), and our Redeemer (v. 22). That's why the old hymn is spot in when it talks of 'When we walk with the Lord, in *the light of His Word.*'[3]

As well as waiting on God and learning from his Word, we need to be confessing our sin. David addresses this twice in the psalm. First in verses 6 and 7, he makes a two-fold plea to God: 'Remember your mercy, O LORD, and your steadfast love ... [but] remember not the sins of my youth or my transgressions.' 'Mercy' is when God does *not* give us what we deserve. How much we need God's mercy! And all the more so when we say with David in verse

> **To belittle the importance of sin belittles what Jesus accomplished for us on the cross.**

11, 'Pardon my guilt, for it is great.' I think we're so often tempted to pray: 'Lord, pardon my sin, but it's only quite small!' But to belittle the importance of sin belittles what Jesus accomplished for us on the cross. Instead, we should honestly confess the vileness of our sin and then throw ourselves upon God's 'steadfast love'—his never-failing, covenant, promise-keeping love.

Fourth, we should be walking in the fear of the Lord (v. 14). But what is 'the fear of the Lord?' Well, it's not a cringing dread of God. It's not a guilty, 'Oh no, here comes God. I'm in for it now!' No! The fear of the Lord is an awesome reverence for God. The nineteenth century theologian Charles Bridges, puts it like this: 'The fear of the

Lord is the affectionate reverence by which the child of God bends himself humbly and carefully to His Father's will.'[4] Do you fear God in that way—with awesome, yet affectionate, reverence? It's only when we have a true understanding of 'the fear of the Lord' that we shall appreciate the glorious paradox of the psalmist in verse 14 that, 'The friendship of the LORD is for those who fear him.'

So far, we've seen that in our daily walk with God we should be waiting on him, learning from his Word, confessing our sin and receiving his merciful forgiveness as well as walking in the fear of the Lord thereby enjoying his friendship. Finally, our walk should be prayerful. David closes the psalm with a prayer in which he recaps many of these themes we have just considered—God's graciousness (v. 16), God's forgiving mercy (v. 18), and of waiting upon God (v. 21). This is to walk in the way of the righteous; this is to find Jesus as 'the way, the truth and the life.'

> O walk with Jesus, wouldst thou know
> How deep, how wide His love can flow!
> They only fail His love to prove,
> Who in the ways of sinners rove.
>
> Jesus, a great desire have we
> To walk life's troubled path with Thee:
> Come to us now, in converse stay;
> And O, walk with us day by day.[5]

REFLECT ON THESE POINTS:

- To belittle the importance of sin belittles what Jesus accomplished for us on the cross.
- 'The fear of the Lord is the affectionate reverence by which the child of God bends himself humbly and carefully to His Father's will.' (Charles Bridges)
- To walk in the way of the righteous is to find Jesus as 'the way, the truth and the life.'

PSALM 26

How firm a foundation

Interviewed on CNN by Larry King in January 1988, the American evangelist Billy Graham talked about what he thought would happen when he died and of his certainty of heaven and eternal life. 'Have you ever doubted?' asked King. 'Never doubted!' replied Graham. If you're seeking assurance of salvation and eternal life you would tend to turn to the New Testament and especially to Paul's second letter to Timothy (1:12; 4:8, 18). You could also turn to the twenty-sixth Psalm where David offers us a four-step guide to assurance—four characteristics that the true Christian should see evidence of in their life.[1]

First, the Christian should be walking with a clear conscience (vv. 1–3). It has been said that 'character is what you do when no one is watching.' But when David says that 'I have walked in my integrity' he knows that God is watching. Indeed, so confident is David of this fact that he invites God to 'prove', 'try' and 'test' him (v. 2). For the believer, integrity is about God, not about us. We know that he knows all about us (Ps. 139:1–6) and it is our life's joy to live for his approval—not to gain salvation, but because he has gained salvation for us. And David, too, knows that it's all because of what God has done—because of 'your steadfast love' and 'your faithfulness' (v. 3).

But before we move on, there is one problem we need to address. For anyone who knows even a little about David's life would want to say to him: 'You talk of your integrity and how certain you are that God will vindicate you, but how can you say that? What about Uriah and Bathsheba? What about your fecklessness with Absalom?' Well let's be clear, David is not behaving like the Pharisees of Jesus' day. He doesn't think he's so much better than all these other 'sinners'. Read Psalm 51! We need to remember what we said earlier about David being not only a king but a prophet and of how, as the apostle Peter put it, 'Being therefore a prophet . . . [David] foresaw and spoke of . . . the Christ' (Acts 2:30–31). The fourth century patriarch, Athanasius of Alexandria (296–373) wrote of how before Christ came among us, 'God sketched the likeness of His perfect life in the Psalms.'[2] So David—like us—can sing verses 1–3 only partially. But we can hear Jesus singing them fully. And if we have his Holy Spirit indwelling our hearts then we can say with the apostle John, 'But if we walk in the light, as he is in the light . . . [then] the blood of Jesus his Son cleanses us from all sin' (1 Jn. 1:7).

Second, the Christian should be practising social distancing (vv. 4–5). As I write this, Britain is emerging from what Prime Minister Boris Johnson called 'our long national hibernation' in which we learnt how to avoid other people as never before because of the Covid-19 pandemic. We even coined the polite phrase of 'social distancing'. And the godly person needs to distance themselves from 'the men of falsehood', the 'hypocrites', the 'evildoers' and 'the wicked'. When David says that he doesn't 'sit' with such folk, he doesn't mean that literally. He means that he doesn't belong with them, she doesn't identify with them, he doesn't count himself as one of them, she doesn't share their values. This is not a plea for monasticism. But it is a plea for godly, distinctive living. Do you feel uncomfortable in the ungodly world? You should. And if you do, take assurance that here is another sign of your being one whose life is pleasing to God.

Do you feel uncomfortable in the ungodly world? You should.

Third, the Christian should possess a godly delight in the company of God's people (vv. 6–8). In verses 6 and 7, David sings of his delight in the worship of God. In the context of Jewish worship, the altar was where the sin offerings were made, and in our Christian setting we are remembering the place where our great, once for all time, sin offering was made. The writer to the Hebrews reminds us in talking of Christ that 'by a single offering he has perfected for all time those who are being sanctified' (Heb. 6:14). Then in verse 8, having told us earlier what he hates, David now tells us what he loves. 'I love the habitation of your house and the place where your glory dwells.' As Michael Wilcock puts it: 'David distances himself from one assembly and associates himself with another.'[3] David speaks in Old Testament language—of the tabernacle or the temple being 'the place where [God's] glory dwells' (v. 8). For as Paul asks the Corinthian Christians, 'Do you not know that you are God's temple and that God's Spirit dwells in you?' And the 'you' in that question is plural. So Paul is referring to the gathering together of Christian believers—the church. So as we sing Psalm 26:8, we are saying that we love—not the building—but being anywhere where Christ's true followers gather together, that we love being in the company of believers. But there is a note of caution needed here for there is a danger in today's church that this intimacy of God, through his Holy Spirit, actually coming to live among his people, can quickly turn into casualness. Alec Motyer rightly warns us:

> The homeliness of God taking an earthly address, and the intimacy of his actually coming to live among his people, must never degenerate into casualness. He is with us in all his glory; in the fullness of his holiness. The place on which we stand is holy ground and without the precious blood of atonement we dare not enter his presence.[4]

A clear conscience, a necessary distance, a godly delight

should all be the hallmarks of the Christian. They are all things that, if we honestly possess them through God's grace, then they will build up our Christian assurance. But there's a fourth characteristic which is somewhat out of fashion these days, what Christopher Ash calls a 'healthy horror' of God's final judgement (vv. 9–10). Now here's a paradox, that such a horror deepens our assurance whereas shallow, superficial Christianity has no such horror. 'Do not sweep me away with sinners, nor my life with bloodthirsty men,' David prays (v. 9). Revelation 6:15–16 speaks of a truly awful scene at which true Christians shudder, because they know it's true.

So what do all these things add up to for David? 'My foot stands on level ground,' he tells us (v. 12). Do you have this firm assurance of sins forgiven, of a certain hope of eternal life? If you do, then you too have your feet on 'level ground.' And only God's Word can give us that foundation.

> How firm a foundation, ye saints of the Lord,
> Is laid for your faith in His excellent Word;
> What more can He say than to you He hath said,
> You who unto Jesus for refuge have fled?[5]

REFLECT ON THESE POINTS:

- For the believer, integrity is about God, not about us. We know that he knows all about us and it is our life's joy to live for his approval—not to gain salvation, but because he has gained salvation for us.

- Do you feel uncomfortable in the ungodly world? You should. And if you do, take assurance that here is another sign of your being one whose life is pleasing to God.
- 'The homeliness of God taking an earthly address, and the intimacy of his actually coming to live among his people, must never degenerate into casualness. He is with us in all his glory; in the fullness of his holiness.' (Alec Motyer)

PSALM 27

Jesus, my strength, my hope

On 28 October 1885, James Hannington—the first Anglican Bishop in Uganda and a distant relative on my mother's side—was in prison awaiting certain death. The following day he would be killed, martyred for his Christian faith aged just 38. And there in a rat-infested jail in south-eastern Uganda, Bishop Hannington wrote these words in his daily diary: 'I am quite broken down and brought very low. Comforted by reading Psalm 27.'[1] And my prayer is that we might be both comforted, and challenged, by this psalm. It's a psalm with four stanzas. It's also a psalm to which two words are the key: 'confidence' and 'seek'. The first and last stanzas speak of David's confidence in God; the middle two stanzas speak of David seeking God.

The first stanza (vv. 1–3) opens with a real blockbuster of a start. It's as if the opening line of Shakespeare's *Hamlet* had been: 'To be, or not to be, that is the question'! David makes this dramatic, three-fold assertion of God as his light, his salvation and his stronghold, what Calvin calls 'this triple shield' of divine protection. 'The LORD is my light and my salvation; whom shall I fear? The LORD is the stronghold of my life; of whom shall I be afraid?'

Here are three more descriptions of God's character to add to David's opening of Psalm 23, 'The LORD is my shepherd; I shall not want.' Now these three words—light, salvation, stronghold—held spiritual meaning even to the Old Testament believer. But how much more wonderful they are for the Christian. 'God is my light,' says David— and our minds go to Jesus' words: 'I am the light of the world. Whoever follows me will never walk in darkness, but will have the light of life' (Jn. 8:12). Salvation speaks of deliverance and rescue. And we hear the writer to the Hebrews talking of how Jesus 'became the source of eternal salvation for all who obey him' (Heb. 5:9). And thirdly my stronghold (v. 2)—and this speaks of refuge and security. Jesus says of all true believers, 'I give them eternal life, and they shall never perish; no one can snatch them out of my hand' (Jn. 10:28). And it's this 'triple shield' that causes David to ask his rhetorical question: 'Whom shall I fear?' with the implied answer of 'nothing, no-one of any eternal consequence,' and surely that's a truth to hold on to in our uncertain days.

But we've not yet acknowledged the most important word in these verses—the word 'my'. And it warns us not to become, as it were, spiritual travel agents! Because some travel agents get so used to talking about places they've never actually been to, that they begin to think—and even talk—as if they have been there! And sadly it's possible to be so used to talking of spiritual things but it's all second-hand. So David here challenges us: Is the Lord Jesus Christ *my* light, *my* salvation and *my* refuge? If he is, then the end of verse 3 is true: 'Though war arise against me, yet will I be confident.'

Then in the second stanza (vv. 4–6), David sings of his seeking God in worship. David writes in verse 4: 'One thing have I asked of the LORD.' Now if God offered today to give you one thing, what would you ask for? And the one thing David asked God for is 'that I may dwell in the house of the LORD all the days of my life.' But it's actually not *the building* that David is obsessed with, but rather *the God* who is there. Again verse 4: 'To gaze upon the beauty of the LORD.' Do we share that wonder of God and his beauty? And for the Christian, God dwells not in a building but in your heart, by his Holy Spirit. And that's why we should want to worship him, or as David has it in verse 6: 'to sing and make melody to the LORD.'

If God offered today to give you one thing, what would you ask for?

Suddenly, the mood changes from joyful praise to earnest prayer. And in the six verses of the third stanza (vv. 7–12) David talks of seeking God in trials, and he makes a catalogue of requests to God. And through all his trials, David is seeking God. He talks with God: 'You have said, "Seek my face." My heart says to you "Your face, LORD, do I seek"' (v. 8). And here David is claiming God's promise, quoting it back to God in prayer, and as it were saying to God, 'Do as you have said!' And it's a wonderful way to use Scripture in our prayers, especially in the midst of our trials.

And then in verse 10 this heartfelt truth: 'For my father and mother have forsaken me, but the LORD will take me in,' or as one commentator has it, 'the Lord will adopt me as *his* child!'[2] And God as our heavenly parent is a wonderfully rich biblical theme. In Psalm 103, David writes that, 'As a father shows compassion to his children, so the LORD shows compassion to those who fear him' (Ps. 103:13). And God, speaking through the prophet Isaiah, asks: 'Can a woman forget her nursing child, that she should have no compassion on the son of her womb?' And he immediately replies: 'Even these may forget, yet I will not forget you' (Is. 49:15). As one of our much-loved hymns puts it, asking the same question and giving the same wonderful and gracious answer:

> Can a woman's tender care
> Cease towards the child she bare?
> Yes, she may forgetful be,
> Yet will I remember thee.

And then God, as it were, speaks as he tells us:

> Mine is an unchanging love,
> Higher than the heights above,

171

Deeper than the depths beneath,
Free and faithful, strong as death.[3]

And so David comes full circle, back to his confidence in God: 'I am still confident of this: I will see the goodness of the LORD in the land of the living' (v. 13, NIV). And here we have a hint of the final resurrection and an echo of Job writing centuries early: 'For I *know* that my Redeemer lives, and at the last he will stand upon the earth. And after my skin has been thus destroyed, yet in my flesh I shall see God' (Job 19:25–26). But for that we must 'wait'. 'Wait for the LORD,' writes David, 'and let your heart take courage; wait for the LORD' (v. 14). Waiting is often the most difficult of spiritual disciplines to learn. But God commands it. That's what Bishop Hannington did, and the psalm that so encouraged and comforted him bids us do the same: 'Be strong and take heart and wait, I say, for the LORD.'

Jesus, my strength, my hope,
On Thee I cast my care;
With humble confidence look up,
And know Thou hearest prayer.
Give me on Thee to wait
Till I can all things do;
On Thee, almighty to create,
Almighty to renew.[4]

REFLECT ON THESE POINTS:

- David asks his rhetorical question: 'Whom shall I fear?' with the implied answer of 'nothing, no-one of any eternal consequence,' and surely that's a truth to hold on to in our uncertain days.
- Claiming God's promise, quoting it back to God in prayer, and as it were saying to God, 'Do as you have said!' is a wonderful way to use Scripture in our prayers, especially in the midst of our trials.

PSALM 28

Inspirer and hearer of prayer

At the close of Psalm 27 David bid us 'wait for the LORD.' Well, at the start of Psalm 28, David has obviously been following his own teaching for he has clearly been praying to God for deliverance for some time—and he's still waiting for God to answer. Indeed, he's wondering if God has even heard him. And if you've been a Christian believer for any length of time, you'll probably know that experience too. Something we all have to learn is that God doesn't usually respond to our prayer on *our* timetable.

I recently came across a folded piece of paper in the King James Bible I used to use each day. It's dated 3–4 January 1981 and details a night I spent in prayer for some very specific things that were troubling me at that time. (I do have to admit that I can't remember spending any other night in prayer to God.) On it, I had listed the things I would pray for and looking at them all these years later, three stand out. One of these prayers God answered—in February 2002. He answered another—in December 2006, over 25 years later! As for a third, I'm still waiting for the answer for which I prayed, but I think in my heart I know what the Lord's answer has been: 'My grace is sufficient for you, for my power is made perfect in weakness' (2 Cor.

12:9). I suspect you know how David felt when he penned these words: 'To you, O LORD, I call; my rock, be not deaf to me, lest, if you be silent to me, I become like those who go down to the pit' (Ps. 28:1). You too may know the experience of what Dale Ralph Davis calls 'the silence we dread.'[1] We need to pray with the hymn writer of old for:

> Patience to watch and wait and weep,
> Though mercy long delay.[2]

And we need to come to God on the same basis as does David in verse 2. 'I lift up my hands towards your most holy sanctuary,' says David. He's referring to the holy of holies where the high priest went once a year to sprinkle the atoning blood on the Ark of the Covenant for the people's sins. David, of course, never went in there, but by faith he believes that his prayers do! So David comes to God on the basis of the blood shed for his sins. And we can come to God only through the blood shed for our sins by Christ on the cross at Calvary. There is no other basis for pleading our prayers in the throne room of God.

Then in the second stanza of the psalm David presents his plea (vv. 3–5). It's a plea for God's retribution against 'the wicked' (v. 3), a group of people we've heard a lot about in these early psalms. The trouble is when we hear that term, we tend to think of people who commit murder, terrorists, drug dealers or the like. But according to verse 3, the wicked are hypocrites—people who 'speak peace with their neighbours while evil is in their hearts.' God hates hypocrisy. And we can all too easily forget that he sees everything and knows everything about us—even our thoughts. David therefore prays that their evil deeds will boomerang on themselves (v. 4a), that God will 'give them according to the work of *their hands* ... because they do not regard the work of *[the Lord's]* hands' (vv. 4–5).

Now this kind of language in the psalms makes many a reader uncomfortable. After all, Jesus teaches: 'Judge not, that you be not judged' (Matt. 7:1), and prays for the forgiveness of his tormentors (Lk. 23:34). But we need to keep in mind first that David is not concerned about their sin against him so much as their sin against God (v. 5). Second, David is not speaking as a private individual but as Israel's anointed king (v. 8). And third, David is acting biblically. He's agreeing with the verse that Paul alludes to in Romans 12:19—'Vengeance is mine, I will repay, says the Lord.'[3] We need to remember just how revolting our sin is to our holy God and the consequences that un-confessed and un-pardoned sin will bring.

We need to remember just how revolting our sin is to our holy God.

In the psalm's third stanza (vv. 6–7), David gives thanks to God 'for he has heard the voice of my pleas for mercy'— an almost word-for-word repeat of his original prayer in verse 2. As Derek Thomas writes: 'Let the truth that God hears our prayers be an encouragement to you. Do not allow the voice of the Evil One to suggest that God is not interested in your heartfelt cries.'[4]

In Psalm 23, David told us that 'the LORD is my shepherd.' In Psalm 27, he told us that 'the LORD is my light and my salvation.' Here in Psalm 28, David gives thanks to God, for he is 'my strength and my shield' (v. 7). What a wonderful privilege prayer is, and how good to know that whatever we may feel at the time, God does hear and, in his own time and in his own sovereign plan, he answers. But do we pray? We read of the early church that 'they devoted themselves to the apostles' teaching and the fellowship, to the breaking of bread and the prayers' (Acts 2:42). R.A. Torrey in his classic book on the subject of prayer writes:

What a wonderful privilege prayer is.

> We do not live in a praying age ... We live in an age of hustle and bustle, of man's efforts and man's determination, and man's confidence in himself and in his own power to achieve things.[5]

The years that have passed since Torrey wrote those words have not, I think, much altered their relevance. We need to be challenged as to whether we are truly men and women of prayer.

Thus far, the psalm has been personal. But now in the

177

final stanza (vv. 8–9), David extends his prayer to include all of God's people thereby giving the psalm a corporate conclusion. It reminds us that our prayers should never focus exclusively on the personal. And the final verse is a gem—what Matthew Henry calls 'a comprehensive prayer for the church of God.'[6] Back in Psalm 16 we thought about the wonderful inheritance that the Christian has in God: 'The lines have fallen for me in pleasant places; indeed, *I* have a beautiful inheritance' (Ps. 16:6). But now in Psalm 28, David wonderfully describes us as God's inheritance! 'Oh, save your people and bless *your* heritage!' (v. 9). In the Hebrew, the word rendered 'inheritance' in Psalm 16:6 and 'heritage' in Psalm 28:9 is the same. So what a wonderful truth is this, that just as our inheritance and portion is God, so God's inheritance and portion is his people!

Then, in the final line, David again likens God to the divine shepherd of which he spoke so memorably in the opening line of the twenty-third Psalm. 'Be their shepherd,' he prays, 'and carry them forever.' And in those painful, dark, lonely moments, God comes to us and tells us: 'Even to your old age I am he, and to grey hairs I will carry you. I have made, and I will bear; I will carry and will save you' (Is. 46:4).

> Inspirer and hearer of prayer,
> Both leading and guarding your sheep,

I place in your covenant care
My life, both awake and asleep;
If you are my shield and my sun
The night is no darkness to me,
For, fast as my moments roll on,
So nearer to you I shall be.[7]

Reflect on these points:

- Something we all have to learn is that God doesn't usually respond to our prayer on our timetable.
- We need to remember just how revolting our sin is to our holy God and to the consequences that un-confessed and un-pardoned sin will bring.
- 'Let the truth that God hears our prayers be an encouragement to you. Do not allow the Evil One to suggest that God is not interested in your heartfelt cries.' (Derek Thomas)

PSALM 29

The deep thunder clouds form

Just when maybe you're thinking that Psalms are a bit 'samey' up pops Psalm 29 which is quite unlike its twenty-eight predecessors. It's a psalm that consists entirely of praise to God. It's also pure poetry. Yes, I know all psalms are poetry but this is so vivid, so pictorial, so colourful in its language and expression. It's a poem with sound effects—thundering, breaking, flashing, shaking. As Charles Spurgeon suggests, if Psalm 8 is best read under a starlit sky, then Psalm 29 is best read during a stupendous thunderstorm. The Canadian theologian of the last century Harry Ironside (1876–1951) called it 'probably the finest poem in the Bible and one of the loveliest poems I have ever seen.'[1] It's arranged in three unequal stanzas with a two-verse introduction and a two-verse conclusion either side of the main theme in verses 3–9. And although the works of nature feature prominently, especially in that middle stanza, David's focus is not on the creation so much as the Creator—the Lord, Jehovah—who is named eighteen times in the psalm's eleven verses. He doesn't want us to miss that!

The brief introduction is a call to worship God—but not to his fellow human beings but to the 'heavenly beings'

(v. 1). They are bidden to ascribe 'glory' to God—'the glory due his name' (v. 2). And that is why we should worship him too, because he is worthy of our worship. There's the possibility of some misunderstanding in verse 2 when David bids us 'worship the LORD in the splendour of holiness.' But the 'splendour' and the 'holiness' are both his, not ours. We are not being told to worship God in a Gothic cathedral or with beautiful liturgy—*our* presumed splendour and holiness—but, as the Wycliffe Bible suggests, to 'worship the LORD in the beauty of *his* holiness.' This is why later in the psalm the temple worshippers will 'all cry "Glory!"' (v. 9).

Now imagine playing Beethoven's *Sixth Symphony* to someone who knows nothing about it and has never heard it before and then asking them what they think of it. They might say they liked it, or they didn't like it. But what if you then asked them if they *understood* it? 'It's a piece of music,' they'd probably reply. 'What is there to *understand* about it?' But if you then told them that Beethoven wrote it as a kind of musical picture of life in the countryside and that it has movements (parts) called 'Scene by the Brook', 'Storm' and 'Shepherd's Song after the Storm' they would surely much better understand Beethoven's *Pastoral Symphony*.

Well it's much the same with the main stanza of Psalm 29. You can't really understand it until someone tells you that David is painting a poetic picture of a mighty thunderstorm. You may well be asking how that works; after all the word 'thunder' appears only once in the entire psalm (v. 3). Yes, but this is *poetry*. So what's the oft-repeated word or phrase of verses 3–9? Well, that's obvious—'The voice of the LORD.' It comes seven times in these seven verses. But what's the connection between a great thunderstorm and 'the voice of the LORD'? Now that's a very good question! And you'll find the answer elsewhere in the Bible.

What's the connection between a great thunderstorm and 'the voice of the LORD'?

When Moses went up Mount Sinai to receive the Ten Commandments, what did the Children of Israel see and hear? Exodus 20:18 tells us that 'when all the people saw the thunder and the flashes of lightning . . . the people were afraid.' When in the time of Samuel the Philistines came and attacked Israel what happened? First Samuel 7:10 tells us that as Samuel was offering the sacrifice and the Philistines were on the point of attacking, 'the LORD thundered with a mighty sound against the Philistines and threw them into confusion, and they were defeated before Israel.' So thunder and lightning are here representing God's presence, God's glory, God's judgement—God's voice! That's what the poetry of Psalm 29 is portraying.

There's one further piece of the puzzle we need to

182

know—the geography. This isn't just any thunderstorm. Not only is it the most spectacular storm you've ever seen, but it's occurring in a specific location. It starts brewing 'over the waters' (v. 3)—the eastern Mediterranean. Then it comes ashore in Lebanon—Israel's northern neighbour—in verse 5. By verse 6 it's racing south, where it makes 'Sirion [to skip] like a young wild ox'—and Sirion is another name for Mount Carmel. Now the storm has reached the northern parts of Israel and is of truly spectacular proportions with quite devastating effects. Mighty cedar trees are broken (v. 5), and our English translators manage a wonderful piece of alliteration in verse 7: 'The voice of the LORD flashes forth flames of fire.' The deer is so startled and frightened that she gives premature birth, and the forests are 'stripped bare' (v. 9a). By now the storm has torn through the length of the whole country, before it 'shakes the wilderness of Kadesh' (verse 8)—on the southern border with Egypt—and the land gasps! And what is the only rational response to such divine power? 'And in his temple all cry "Glory!"' (v. 9b):

> O tell of His might, O sing of His grace,
> Whose robe is the light, whose canopy space.
> His chariots of wrath the deep thunder-clouds
>   form,
> And dark is His path on the wings of the storm.[2]

Rather like Beethoven, David seems to want to end

with a peaceful song after the storm. Some see echoes here of God's 'still small voice' (1 Kgs. 19:12, KJV) after the earthquake, wind and fire on Mount Horeb. The nineteenth century German theologian Franz Delitzsch (1813–90) somewhat ingeniously saw the short two-verse stanzas at each end of the psalm as representing *Gloria in excelsis Deo* (vv. 1–2) and *Pax in terris* (vv. 10–11) pointing forward to the angelic song at the birth of Christ: 'Glory to God in the highest, and on earth peace among those with whom he is pleased!' (Lk. 2:14). But as Spurgeon concludes: 'Power was displayed in the hurricane whose course the psalm so grandly pictures; and now, in the cool calm after the storm, that power is promised to be the strength of God's chosen people.'[3]

The danger today is that God too easily becomes a chum, a mate. But as Gerald Wilson points out, 'When Isaiah saw that "Holy, holy, holy is the LORD God Almighty" (Is. 6:3) he did not grin and slap God on the back. He didn't even give him a friendly hug or handshake. Rather, he found himself prostrate on the ground.' He continues: 'When we really see God as he is—when his power and holiness is displayed for us—there should be no other appropriate response but to get on our knees in acknowledgement of just how far our lives, even at their very best, are removed from the holiness of God and just how undeserved is the gracious love and salvation that God pours out on us day by day.'[4]

O measureless Might, ineffable Love,
While angels delight to hymn Thee above,
Thy humbler creation, though feeble their lays,
With true adoration shall sing to Thy praise.[5]

REFLECT ON THESE POINTS:

- The reason why we should worship God is because he is worthy of our worship.
- 'When we really see God as he is—when his power and holiness is displayed for us—there should be no other appropriate response but to get on our knees in acknowledgement of just how far our lives, even at their very best, are removed from the holiness of God and just how undeserved is the gracious love and salvation that God pours out on us day by day.' (Gerald Wilson)

Psalm 30

Mornings of joy

Psalm 30 is in a very similar form to its predecessor—an introduction (vv. 1–5), a conclusion (vv. 11–12) and the main subject of the psalm in the middle stanza (vv. 6–10). In its shape, Psalm 30 is rather like a fairground big dipper! In verse 1, David is 'drawn up' but in verse 3 there are 'those who go down'. In verse 5, we have God's 'anger' followed by God's 'favour', 'a moment' followed by 'a lifetime', 'weeping' followed by 'joy', 'night' followed by 'the morning'. Even towards the psalm's conclusion we have 'mourning' turning into 'dancing', and 'sackcloth' exchanged for 'gladness' (v. 11). Here is a psalm of opposites, what James Boice calls 'a litany of uplifting contrasts.'[1] This poses the all-important questions. First, why was David, figuratively and spiritually, in a pit, facing God's anger, weeping and clothed in sackcloth? And second, how and why was he drawn out of that pit, enjoying God's favour, joyful and clothed with gladness? Third, how does this all apply to you and me today?

But before we can answer those questions, we need to know something about the background to David's writing of this psalm, and that's where things get a bit tricky. The superscription of the psalm reads: 'A Psalm of David. A

186

Song at the Dedication of the Temple' (ESV). The trouble is that the Hebrew word rendered here as 'temple' can also mean 'house', and thus the New King James Version has 'A Song at the Dedication of the house.' Now David's death is recorded in 1 Kings 2, whilst the building of the temple doesn't even start until the fourth year of Solomon's reign (1 Kings 6:1) and took seven years to build (1 Kings 6:38). True, David could have written this psalm in anticipation of the Temple's dedication but that seems less likely than that the setting of this psalm is the dedication of David's own house.[2]

So what was going on in David's life around the time when his own house (palace) in Jerusalem was being built? The inspired writer tells us a number of things. First, 'David grew stronger and stronger' in relation to Ish-bosheth, the son of Saul who had been made king over the northern tribes (2 Sam. 3:1). Second, he had six children by six different wives (2 Sam. 3:2–5). Third, there was his treatment of his former wife Michal whom he treats as a bargaining chip to strengthen his claim to the throne of all Israel. David had loved her once but now he broke up her marriage with Paltiel who was clearly devoted to her (2 Sam. 3:14–16) only then to keep her under virtual house arrest in his harem and she remained childless (2 Sam. 6:23). Finally, by his behaviour towards Ish-bosheth, David promoted civil war between Judah and Israel with dreadful consequences for the future, creating the fault line along which the whole nation would one day break apart.[3]

It's against that background that David writes in Psalm 30: 'As for me, I said in my prosperity, "I shall never be moved"' (v. 6). What 'a foolish boast,' as Derek Kidner calls it.[4] But how often is it true of us that in times of prosperity, ease and success we are tempted to become spiritually complacent, drifting away from God and forgetting that he is the Provider of everything we have. It's no new sin! God warned his people of it even before they entered the Promised Land:

> Take care lest you forget the LORD your God . . . lest
> when you have eaten and are full and have built
> good houses and live in them, and when your herds
> and flocks multiply and your silver and gold is
> multiplied and all that you have is multiplied, then
> your heart be lifted up, and you forget the LORD
> your God . . . Beware lest you say in your heart, 'My
> power and the might of my hand have gotten me
> this wealth' (Deut. 8:11–17).

And like the Children of Israel, and like David, we forget! Just note the self-satisfaction, self-centredness and complacency of verse 6: 'As for me, I said in my prosperity, "I shall never be moved."' But then God 'hides his face' and we, like David, are 'dismayed' (v.7). We thought we had everything worked out, everything planned, everything under our control, and then—the loved one is taken, your health is threatened, the job is gone, or whatever it is God is pleased to use in his grace to bring us to our senses. For me it was a sudden diagnosis of cancer in February 2002. But God used the furnace of that affliction to bring me back to himself. The eighteenth century cleric John Berridge (1716–93) was right when he remarked: 'A Christian never falls asleep in the fire or in the deep water, but grows drowsy in the sunshine.' Can you say with the psalmist: 'Before I was afflicted I went astray, but now I keep your word'? (Ps. 119:67).

It is only because of God's grace and mercy that the Lord does not abandon us to our complacency.

That's why David now wants to look back on this experience—this brush with death (vv. 1–3)—and praise his merciful God. 'For his anger is but for a moment, and his favour is for a lifetime' (v. 5a). God is rightly angered at our sin. His anger is just and reflects his perfect holiness. But as Alec Motyer so beautifully expresses it: 'It is the Lord's nature to (if we may put it like this) tip the balance in the direction of "favour" and away from "anger". All the time—again if we may put it this way—mercy is clamouring to triumph over justice.'[5] This is wonderfully shown in the life of

189

Hezekiah who, like David, 'became sick and was at the point of death' (Is. 38:1). Hezekiah prays for mercy and God, through Isaiah, tells him: 'I have heard your prayer; I have seen your tears. Behold I will add fifteen years to your life' (Is. 38:5). And, like David, Hezekiah breaks forth into a wonderful psalm of praise (Is. 38:10–20).

Back in Psalm 30, then come the lines for which the psalm is best known and loved: 'Weeping may tarry for the night, but joy comes with the morning' (v. 5b). The Hebrew word rendered 'tarry' is one used to describe the activity of an overnight guest, a wayfarer, one 'who comes in at evening to lodge for the night.'[6] In a more literal translation, therefore, the second half of verse 5 would read: 'In the evening, weeping may come in to pass the night; but at dawn [there is] a shout of joy.'[7] Perowne comments: 'Just as the sun in Eastern lands, without any long prelude of twilight to announce its coming, leaps as it were in a moment above the horizon, so does the light of God's love dispel in a moment the long night and darkness of sorrow.'[8] And in the New Testament, Jesus adds an eternal perspective to this anticipated joy when he tells his disciples before his crucifixion: 'So also you have sorrow now, but I will see you again, and your hearts will rejoice, and no one will take your joy from you' (Jn. 16:22). Each true believer can pray this prayer in the words of the nineteenth century minister and hymn writer John Monsell:

> Mornings of joy give for evenings of tearfulness,
> Trust for our trembling and hope for our fear.[9]

REFLECT ON THESE POINTS:

- How often is it true of us that in times of prosperity, ease and success we are tempted to become spiritually complacent, drifting away from God and forgetting that he is the Provider of everything we have.
- 'A Christian never falls asleep in the fire or in the deep water, but grows drowsy in the sunshine.' (John Berridge)

PSALM 31

My times are in Thy hand

Here we have a psalm of lament which displays such a wide range of human emotions and spiritual temperatures. Here is an aching heart and yet also a trusting heart. But what is unusual about this psalm is that David goes from lament to trust and praise not once, but twice. He begins with a plea for God's help in difficult times but by verses 7 and 8 David is rejoicing and praising God for his deliverance. But then in verse 9, he seems to start all over again before, for a second time, coming back to praise God for his mighty deliverance. Were these two different times of trial following one upon another, or are verses 9–24 a kind of amplification of the pleas of the first eight verses? As this is one of the longer psalms in Book I of the Psalter, we will spend much of our time in three key verses rather than trying to cover all twenty-four—verses 5, 15 and 24.

David begins with familiar truths—God as his 'rock of refuge' and 'strong fortress' (vv. 2–4). God has rescued him from the net that his enemies had laid to catch him. Our minds go back to the years David spent escaping from King Saul's paranoiac pursuits (1 Samuel 18–31). But David has learnt to trust his faithful God and so he sings: 'Into your hand I commit my spirit; you have redeemed me, O Lord, faithful God' (v. 5). This is one of the psalms in which we come across what we grandly call 'anthropomorphism' as David ascribes human form to God the Father. As Jesus told the Samaritan woman by the well, 'God is *spirit*' (Jn. 4:24), not a human being. So whereas Luke can tell us in his gospel that, quite literally, 'Jesus stretched out his *hand* and touched' the leper (Lk. 5:13), we cannot take David's reference to God's hand in verse 5 of this psalm in a literal sense.

In the Old Testament, there are numerous references to God's hand or 'the hand of the Lord' and it signifies a variety of God's actions and powers. Often God's hand indicates God's judgement—against the Egyptians (Ex. 9:3), against the Philistines (1 Sam. 5:6) and even against his own chosen people as in 'the hand of the Lord was against them' (Deut. 2:15). But it can also indicate God's deliverance, most notably in delivering Israel out of Egypt as when we read that 'the Lord brought [Israel] out of Egypt with a mighty hand' (Deut. 26:8). In a later psalm, the psalmist speaks of God's role in creation by telling us that 'Of old you laid the foundation of the earth, and the heavens are the work of your hands' (Ps. 102:25). It can also reference God's revelation as when Ezekiel tells us that 'the hand of the Lord was upon me' just before he relates the vision of the valley of dry bones (Ezek. 37:1).

Judgement, deliverance, creation and revelation—all by 'the hand of the LORD.'

So what does David want us to understand when he tells us that he commits his spirit into God's hand? I think he's challenging us to trust in God's sovereignty—in his guidance and protection. We read in Proverbs 21:1 that 'the king's heart is a stream of water in the hand of the LORD; he turns it wherever he will.'

And what is true of the king is true of you and of me. Do you believe that? Do you trust God's sovereign, guiding, protecting, providing hand?

Do you trust God's sovereign, guiding, protecting, providing hand?

But this is not only committing one's spirit into God's hand for now, but for eternity. That's why these words have been the last words spoken by the lips of many a saint and why indeed Luke records them from the lips of Jesus on the Cross (Lk. 23:46). The nineteenth century German theologian Franz Delitzsch (1813–90) likens David—and the Christian today—giving his spirit over into God's hand 'as a trust or deposit,' for he adds, 'whatsoever is deposited there is safely kept, and freed from all danger and all distress.'[1] If you do, then like David, you will 'rejoice and be glad in [God's] steadfast love' (v. 7) knowing that he has 'seen my affliction' and 'known the distress of my soul' (v. 7).

194

But then from verse 9, David is again in lament experiencing distress, grief, sorrow, sighing and failing strength (vv. 9–10). Neighbours are forsaking him whilst others conduct whispering campaigns, plots and schemes against him (vv. 11–13). You may well have been through similar distress. It's the way of the world, and if we're living as Christ's followers in a hostile world, we should not be surprised. But in this second bout of depression, David again finds refuge in God. 'But I trust in you, O LORD; I say, "You are my God"' (v. 14). And this second expression of trust leads David to a second reference to the hand of God. 'My times are in your hand,' he states in verse 15—another declaration of God's sovereignty over his life. David talks of his 'times' being in God's hand: the word is plural. So what times are these? And I think the answer is 'all times'—infancy, childhood, youth, maturity and old age. It was this verse that inspired the nineteenth century hymn writer William Lloyd (1791–1853) to write:

If we're living as Christ's followers in a hostile world, we should not be surprised.

> My times are in Thy hand,
> My God, I wish them there;
> My life, my friends, my soul I leave
> Entirely to Thy care.

And the beauty of this hymn is that is helps us to read Psalm 31 from a Christian perspective as he links the figurative hand of God written about by David with the very real hand of Jesus pierced for the believer on the cross at Calvary:

> My times are in Thy hand,
> Jesus the crucified;
> The hand my cruel sins had pierced
> Is now my guard and guide.[2]

Back in Psalm 27 we thought of how good it is to pray through the very words of Scripture, and that's what David does in verse 16, using the words of Aaron's blessing (Num. 6:25) as he prays that God would 'make your face shine on your servant.' And so for a second time in this psalm, David finds his way out of his lament by recalling the character and attributes of God. What an unrivalled recipe that is for the believer caught in hard times. David here recalls God's 'abundant goodness' (v. 19) and his 'steadfast love' (v. 21), wonderful attributes of God that never fail to restore our souls. David's soul is also revived by remembering what God has already done for him—'You heard the voice of my pleas for mercy when I cried to you for help' (v. 22).

Finally, David—as he has before—ends this intensely personal psalm with a call to corporate worship, a call to 'all his saints' (v. 23), to 'all who wait for the LORD' (v. 24).

As one commentator writes: 'They are to wait patiently, for this waiting has a glorious end as the bright spring sun at length breaks through the dark angry aspects of the heavens.'[3]

> My times are in Thy hand;
> I'll always trust in Thee,
> And after death at Thy right hand
> I shall for ever be.

REFLECT ON THESE POINTS:

- When David tells us that he commits his spirit into God's hand, he's challenging us to trust in God's sovereignty—in his guidance and protection.
- David finds his way out of his lament by recalling the character and attributes of God. What an unrivalled recipe that is for the believer caught in hard times.

PSALM 32

God is our guide

Psalm 32 is a psalm about the blessedness—the happiness, the sheer joy—that we can find through having our sins forgiven by God and falls into four stanzas. In verses 1–2, David writes of the God who blesses. When the American colonies declared their independence from Great Britain, the famous Declaration of Independence stated that 'all men are created equal, that they are endowed by their Creator with certain unalienable rights, that among these are life, liberty *and the pursuit of happiness.*'

But David tells us that true happiness, or blessedness, is only for the person whose 'transgression is forgiven, whose sin is covered' (v. 1) and the one 'against whom the LORD counts no iniquity' (v. 2). Those three words—transgression, sin and iniquity—refer, respectively, to our rebellion against God, our falling short of God's mark, and our corrupt nature.[1] Now all that doesn't sound like the source of happiness. No, because that's the bad news. But the good news is what God does with our transgressions, our sin and our iniquity. For David tells us that God deals with our three-fold sin problem with a three-fold solution. They are forgiven, covered (v. 1) and not counted against us (v. 2). 'Forgiven' tells us that our sins have been 'lifted off' us like a load from our back. 'Covered' is a word that is taken from the imagery of the Temple sacrifices when the blood was sprinkled on the Mercy Seat, which was the covering of the Ark of the Covenant, and the blood thereby provided a covering between a Holy God and the broken law. 'Not counted against us' comes from a book-keeping term—and it's the word the apostle Paul uses in Romans to explain how God writes our sin into Christ's ledger and punishes it in him, while at the same time writing the righteousness of Christ into our ledger and counting us as justified because of his merit. Forgiven, covered and imputed to Christ—that's what has happened to our sin if we have truly trusted in Christ. Do you truly know that bliss, that happiness?

Now suddenly the mood changes (vv. 3–5) as David recollects a period in his life when his sin went unconfessed. David had committed adultery with Bathsheba, and then arranged the death of her husband Uriah so that he could marry her. And for about a year David had been trying to cover up those sins. And only after Nathan's rebuke (2 Sam. 12:1–12) did David confess his sin. And in verses 3 and 4 David tells us that sin and a guilty conscience sapped his physical strength, his bones literally 'became old', is what the original means. His vitality is gone, his strength is sapped. Sin has a price tag.

But through it, God speaks to David. And so the guilt that God gives is actually a gift of grace.

In Psalm 31, we thought of the significance of 'the hand of the LORD'. And here in verse 4 David tells us that during this time God's 'hand was heavy upon me.' Charles Spurgeon comments: 'Better the world on your shoulders like Atlas, than God's hand on your heart like David.'[2] '*Then* I acknowledged my sin to You and did not cover up my iniquity. I said, "I will confess my transgressions to the LORD"' (v. 5, NIV). There are those three sin words again—sin, iniquity, transgressions. And verse 5 ends triumphantly: 'And you forgave the guilt of my sin' (NIV). There's not even time to begin a new sentence. I confess my transgressions and—immediately—God forgives! Don't you just wonder at the immediacy of it? This is David's great testimony—of the God who forgives.

David wants us to learn from his mistakes.

So we've seen the God who blesses, the God who forgives, now (vv. 6–7), the God who protects. David wants us to learn from his mistakes. 'Don't be a fool. Don't do what I did and not listen to God's warnings. On the evening of 14 April, 1912, Jack Phillips the wireless operator on board *RMS Titanic* was receiving ice warnings from other ships in the mid-Atlantic. But Phillips was trying to send hundreds of backlogged personal messages from passengers aboard

200

the *Titanic*—the Twitter of 100 years ago. So when Cyril Evans, the radio operator on board the nearby *Californian*, sent further ice warnings, Phillips wired back, 'Shut up! Shut up! I'm busy.' Hours later when the *Titanic* had been holed below the waterline by an iceberg, Phillips desperately tried to contact those same ships, but to no avail.[3] And David warns us: 'Don't wait until you're holed below the moral water line to pray, to be in touch with God.' When we're first tempted, then pray. How prone we are when we first hear God's kind and warning voice to say, 'Shut up, I'm busy!' But sin is too big a thing to be handled alone.

How prone we are when we first hear God's kind and warning voice to say, 'Shut up, I'm busy!'

And in verse 7, David tells us why we should pray, because God will act as a hiding place to protect us from trouble. As the American hymn writer William Cushing puts it:

> O safe to the Rock that is higher than I,
> My soul in its conflicts and sorrows would fly;
> So sinful, so weary, Thine, Thine would I be,
> Thou blest Rock of Ages, I'm hiding in Thee.

Have you heeded David's great warning? Are you praying in times of temptation?

In the final stanza (vv. 8–11), we hear of the God who

guides. At this point, both the subject and the speaker change, for the subject is now guidance for the future rather than forgiveness for the past, and the speaker is God rather than David. 'I,' says God, 'I will instruct you and teach you in the way you should go; I will counsel you with my eye upon you' (v. 8). Here is a great promise that God will guide us. So how *does* God guide his people? Look at the verbs in verse 8—instruct, teach, counsel. God puts us in the spiritual schoolroom. The teacher is the Holy Spirit and the textbook is the Bible. No, the Bible won't tell me whether to buy this house, take that job, or marry that person. But it will enable me to set ideals and priorities by training me to ask the right questions. And the most important question is surely, 'What does God want for me?' And Romans 8:29 tells me that God wants you and me to 'be conformed to the image of his Son.' So we can't know God's guidance if we don't read, and study and seek to understand God's Word. And not to read it as a kind of spiritual horoscope, hoping that some verse will leap out of the page at us and answer our most pressing question. Yes, God sometimes does in his grace cause a verse to speak very specifically to us, but never in a way that is untrue to its context.

So here is David's God—the God who blesses, who forgives, who protects and who guides. Are you, am I, receiving his blessing, his forgiveness, his protection and his guidance? If we are, then with David we shall 'be glad in the Lord' and 'shout for joy' (v. 11).

> God is our guide who watches all our way;
> Gently he teaches us our path to find.
> Be not self-willed, like beasts that go astray,
> God will direct our feet and form our mind:
> Mercy embraces us on every side
> With God our joy, our Saviour, strength and guide.[4]

REFLECT ON THESE POINTS:

- True happiness, or blessedness, is only for the person whose 'transgression is forgiven, whose sin is covered' and the one 'against whom the Lord counts no iniquity'.
- David warns us: 'Don't wait until you're holed below the moral water line to pray, to be in touch with God.' When we're first tempted, then pray.
- God puts us in the spiritual schoolroom. The teacher is the Holy Spirit and the textbook is the Bible.

PSALM 33

Maker and monarch and Saviour of all

The noted columnist and broadcaster Bernard Levin (1928–2004) once posed this question: 'Have I time to discover why I was born before I die?' Levin added: 'I am unable to believe it was an accident; and if it wasn't one, it must have a meaning.'[1] He was right. Life does have a meaning and a purpose, and the author of Psalm 33 knows what it is—to worship God, to give him the praise that is his due, because of who he is and what he has done. The worship of God is indeed 'the true believer's most important activity.'[2]

Like a number of recent psalms, Psalm 33 also has an opening (vv. 1–5) and a concluding stanza (vv. 20–22) with its main theme being contained in the verses between. The opening stanza contains four commands to the worshipper—'Shout for joy in the LORD' (v. 1), 'Give thanks to the LORD,' (v. 2), 'Make melody to him' (v. 2), 'Sing to him' (v. 3). It could hardly be more emphatic that our worship must be vertical—it is 'in the LORD', 'to the LORD', and 'to him.' The fad today in too many churches seems to be to stress the horizontal at least as much as—if not more than—the vertical. The psalmist here does not agree. The psalmist does, however, see a strong connection between worship and music. In his helpful and thought-provoking book *What is Worship Music?* Paul S. Jones states that music in worship should agree with these three principles. First, worship music is praise—it should be the biblical response to God's person, God's works and God's Word. Second, worship music is prayer— it should help us approach God rightly. Third, worship music is proclamation—it should teach and preach God's truths to our hearts.[3] And in verses 4 and 5, the psalmist teaches us truths about some of the attributes of God— that he is upright, acts faithfully, loves both righteousness and justice, and fills the earth with his steadfast love. Reason enough to sing praises to God!

As we come to the first of the psalm's two main stanzas, we are bidden to worship the Creator God (vv. 6–9). 'By the word of the LORD the heavens were made, and by the breath of his mouth all their host' (v. 6). Here we have an echo of the repeated words of Genesis 1–'And God said . . .'—coming as they do at the start of each of Creation's days. Our minds go back too to the opening verse of Psalm 19: 'The heavens declare the glory of God, and the sky above proclaims his handiwork.' And this verse also looks forward to the words of John 1: 'In the beginning was the Word, and the Word was with God, and the Word was God. He was in the beginning with God. All things were made through him, and without him was not any thing made that was made' (Jn. 1:1-3). As one commentator writes concerning verse 8 and of our Creator God: 'He need only speak the word and that which He wills comes into being out of nothing.'[4] This is why all the earth is commanded to 'fear the LORD' and 'all the inhabitants of the world stand in awe of him!' (v. 7). As the nineteenth century hymn writer tells us:

> Songs of praise the angels sang,
> Heaven with alleluias rang,
> When creation was begun,
> When God spake and it was done.[5]

Then in verses 10-19 the psalmist bids us worship the Sovereign God who conducts a divine scrutiny of 'the nations', 'the peoples' (v. 10), 'all the children of man', and 'all the inhabitants of the earth' (v. 14). Notice the repeated word 'all' to signify the completeness of God's sovereignty—'*all* generations' (v. 11), '*all* the children of man' (v. 13), '*all* the inhabitants of the earth' (v. 14), *all* their hearts and *all* their deeds (v. 15). Even the supposed 'greats' of this world are useless—*great* armies, *great* strength, *great* might (vv. 16-17). The history of Israel furnishes us with a number of examples where small armies empowered by God defeated the much larger armies of their enemies. And we should keep in mind the words of Hezekiah facing the armed might of the Assyrians and their king Sennacherib: 'Be strong and courageous . . . for the one with us is greater than the one with him' (2 Chron. 32:7, NASB). So the question we need to pose is this: 'Do we live each day as if we truly believe in the Sovereign God?' Here's how one commentator puts it:

Do we live each day as if we truly believe in the Sovereign God?

> Everything that exists, even to the most hidden thing, is encompassed by His omniscience and omnipotence. He exercises an omniscient control over all things, and makes all things subservient to the designs of His plan of the universe, which, so far as His people are concerned, is the plan of salvation. Without Him nothing comes to pass; but through Him everything takes place.[6]

Is this the God in whom we trust?

Also in this stanza, the psalmist uses language that parallels David's reference to the 'hand of the LORD' in Psalm 31 by referring to the 'eye of the LORD' (v. 18), a phrase that also appears both in Psalm 32:8 and Psalm 34:15. Here in Psalm 33, the psalmist elaborates on this thought as he refers to God's 'looking down' (v. 13), 'looking out' (v. 14) and 'observing' (v. 15) the inhabitants of the earth. This image of divine observation is yet another great biblical theme. Just as earlier we referred to the repeated phrase in the Creation narrative, 'And God said . . .' at the start of each of creation's days, so each of these days ended in the biblical narrative with the phrase 'And *God saw* that it was good.' Thus we learn in Psalm 33 that just as the Creator God speaks, so the Sovereign God sees. As the redemptive story continues, we read that God 'saw that the wickedness of man was great in the earth' (Gen. 6:5) and that he 'saw the people of Israel' suffering in Egypt (Ex. 2:25). In both these references we see that God's 'seeing' was a prelude to God's judgement—the flood and the plagues. And maybe that is what's in the psalmist's mind in verses 13–15.

But then in verses 18–19, God's 'seeing' is a sign of his deliverance and protection of 'those who fear him,' of those 'who hope in his steadfast love.' Indeed, in 2 Chronicles 16:9, we read that 'the eyes of the Lord run to and fro throughout the whole earth, to give strong support to those whose heart is blameless towards him.' So how we respond to 'the eye of God' being on us will depend on the state of our hearts. If our hearts are not right with him, then we will fear God's judgement. But if our hearts have been made right with him then we will rest in his protection and ultimate deliverance. Thus the Creator God and the Sovereign God is also the Saviour God. He truly is, in the words of Reginald Heber's famous Epiphany hymn, 'Maker and Monarch and Saviour of all.'[7]

And so the psalm concludes (vv. 20–22) with a trusting hymn of praise to the God who is 'our help and our shield,' rehearsing again some of God's wonderful attributes—his holiness and his steadfast love. We can almost hear an echo here of the closing lines of Saint Ambrose's heart-lifting *Te Deum Laudamus*:

> O Lord, let Thy mercy lighten upon us: as our trust
>   is in Thee.
> O Lord, in Thee have I trusted: let
>   me never be confounded.

REFLECT ON THESE POINTS:

- We should keep in mind the words of Hezekiah facing the armed might of the Assyrians and their king Sennacherib: 'Be strong and courageous ... for the one with us is greater than the one with him' (2 Chron. 32:7, NASB).

- How we respond to 'the eye of God' being on us will depend on the state of our hearts. If our hearts are not right with him, then we will fear God's judgement. But if our hearts have been made right with him then we will rest in his protection and ultimate deliverance.

PSALM 34

O make but trial of his love

We come now to the third psalm in the Psalter the superscription of which specifies the circumstances in the life of David that led to its writing. The previous two—Psalms 3 and 18—related to events in David's life as king. Psalms 51, 60 and 63 also come from that period. But here in Psalm 34 we have the first of six psalms that come from the period in David's life before he became king much of which was spent fleeing from King Saul. Both this psalm and Psalm 56 come from the events recorded in the opening verses of 1 Samuel 21. David has married Michal, one of Saul's daughters, and with the help of some subterfuge on her part (1 Sam. 19:11–17) is on the run from his father-in-law. He runs first to Samuel at Ramah (1 Sam. 19:18) but leaves there—a decision which at least one commentator regards as 'wrong.'[1] His next stop is Nob, an encampment of priests probably only a couple miles north of Jerusalem. Having fled in a hurry David has neither food nor weapons and so Ahimelech the priest provides both—consecrated bread and the sword of Goliath the Philistine champion whom David had killed. With these provisions, David—for reasons we are not told—then crosses the border into Philistine country and

210

seeks protection from Achish (called Abimelech in the title to Psalm 34) king of Gath.

One cannot help but think that this was utterly foolish on David's part—to arrive in Gath, Goliath's home town, clutching the famous sword of the home town hero whom David recently felled and beheaded, seeking political asylum from Israel's sworn enemies. What was he thinking of? It is worth noting that there is no record of either prayer or of seeking God's guidance in this ludicrous scheme. David's cover is soon blown and it becomes widely known in Gath that their new visitor from Israel is none other than he of whom they sang: 'Saul has struck down his thousands, and David his ten thousands' (1 Sam. 21:11). So David, now fearful of reprisals, feigns madness as a cover. The clever ruse works and Achish lets David go. Clever David!

Well, that's one side of the story. But now with time to reflect on his foolishness, David wants to tell us that it wasn't his cunning plan that got him out of Gath, it was God—he 'delivered me from all my fears' (v. 4), he 'saved me out of all my troubles' (v. 6). As Derek Kidner writes: 'this psalm has all the hallmarks of relief and gratitude for a miraculous escape' but wrought not by David but by God's sovereignty and mercy.[2] Are there not times in our lives upon which we look back with huge gratitude when God rescued us from some great calamity? Let us not forget to do what David does here—to sing the Lord's praises.

As with some of the other longer psalms, we shall briefly review the whole psalm before returning to focus on a key verse or passage. The psalm falls neatly into two fairly equal halves. Charles Spurgeon describes the first ten verses as a hymn, whilst likening the last twelve verses to a sermon. Not only are the first ten verses like a great hymn of praise, they also inspired Nahum Tate (1652–1715) and Nicholas Brady (1659–1726) to pen their great hymn, 'Through all the changing scenes of life.' The hymn as it is sung today covers only six of the psalm's first nine verses but their original version—like the psalm—has twenty-two verses!³

> Just think what David had been through, and yet he can sing of the God 'who delivered me from all my fears'.

The first ten verses alternate between personal testimony and calls for corporate worship, so verse 1 begins, 'I will bless the LORD at all times,' whilst verse 3 ends, 'Let us exalt his name together.' And these verses ring with joyful confidence in God. Just think what David had been through, and yet he can sing of the God 'who delivered me from all my fears' (v. 4) and, extending it to others, that 'The angel of the LORD encamps around those who fear him, and delivers them' (v. 7). As Tate and Brady would have us sing:

> The hosts of God encamp around
> The dwellings of the just;
> Deliv'rance He affords to all
> Who on His succour trust.[4]

Indeed, David wants others to see how good God has been to him so that they too spread the word of God's merciful deliverances. As Tate and Brady express it in a now forgotten verse:

> Behold (say they), behold the man
> Whom Providence relieved;
> So dangerously with woes beset;
> So wondrously retrieved![5]

Then in verses 11–22, David preaches his sermon. It's as if he's saying to us, 'Listen to me. Learn from me. The good you enjoy (v. 12) goes hand in hand with the good you do (v. 14).'[6] And as in the two previous psalms, there is reference to God's eyes being 'toward the righteous' as well as 'his ears toward their cry' (v. 15). But how can David, can I, claim to be counted amongst 'the righteous? For David this was through the atoning sacrifices which were the shadows and types anticipating that great atoning Sacrifice of the Lord Jesus Christ—David's greater Son! And for you and me, it is by being clothed

213

in the righteousness of Christ through faith in that same once and for all-time atoning Sacrifice. What wonderful reassurances for whatever today or tonight brings to know that God sees me, God hears me, God knows me. 'Many are the afflictions of the righteous,' says David, 'but the LORD delivers him out of them all' (v. 19), and at death he will indeed do just that.

Before we close, let's return to verse 8, perhaps the best-known and most-loved verse of this psalm. When in 1953 Ralph Vaughan Williams (1872–1958) was asked to compose a short piece of choral music for the coronation service of Queen Elizabeth II, he wrote an exquisite setting of this very verse in the translation by Myles Coverdale:

> O taste and see how gracious the Lord is.
> Blessed is the man that trusteth in him.

To 'taste and see' God's goodness is more than just sampling food at a buffet. It's to prove by experience. It's that you may know for sure 'how gracious the Lord is' and how blessed are those who take refuge in him. The apostle Peter alludes to the verse in his first letter when he longs that his readers 'may grow up into salvation—if indeed you have tasted that the Lord is good' (1 Pet. 2:2–3).[7] And Jesus tells us that 'I am the bread of life; whoever comes to me shall not hunger, and whoever believes in me shall never thirst' (Jn. 6:35). It is from him and his Word that we are to draw our spiritual nourishment—to taste and see.

214

That is why the God-given Word, 'is to be desired not for its own sake, but because it enables us to feed upon its author, and to appropriate His grace.'[8] Are you tasting and seeing?

> O make but trial of His love,
> Experience will decide
> How blest are they, and only they,
> Who in His truth confide.

REFLECT ON THESE POINTS:

- Are there not times in our lives upon which we look back with huge gratitude when God rescued us from some great calamity? Let us not forget to sing the Lord's praises.
- What wonderful reassurances for whatever today or tonight brings to know that God sees me, God hears me, God knows me.

PSALM 35

Thy all-seeing eye

We come now to a genre of psalm that many a contemporary reader finds most difficult—not because it's particularly difficult to understand, but rather because having understood it, we're not sure how to respond or react to it. Psalm 35 is one of the so-called 'imprecatory psalms' in which the writer asks God to pour out judgement on his enemies. And many a contemporary Christian reader wonders whether they should be saying or singing such words when they're at the same time wanting to be mindful of Jesus' teaching to 'love your enemies' (Matt. 5:44). Some explain away psalms such as this by saying that it's just all 'very Old Testament' and that we don't believe in that kind of a God anymore. But that is to deny both the wholeness of the Bible as one story—with one plan of salvation—and also to contradict the doctrine that God is both unchanging and unchangeable. So, briefly, a few things to remember when we read or sing such psalms.

First, most of these psalms were written by David who was speaking not as a private person but as the anointed king and judge of Israel, and as such he was calling on God to execute righteous judgement upon those who, by

216

opposing him, were opposing God. Second, God hates sin and if we are his people so should we. Third, the reason we may find these psalms troubling might be because, not only have we lost sight of the loathsomeness of sin, but also of the utter holiness of God. We may also have forgotten what our own salvation cost Almighty God—the death of his only beloved Son on the cross at Calvary. It does my soul good from time to time to follow the example of Bishop Walsham How (1823–97) and:

> Shut my eyes and try to see
> The cruel nails and crown of thorns,
> And Jesus crucified for me.[1]

Fourth, we should remember that throughout, the Bible makes a clear distinction between those who are for God and those who are against him and the very different end awaiting them at a final judgement. Jesus talks about this as a separating of the sheep from the goats (Matt. 25:31–33). So, as Allan Harman suggests, 'in appealing for God's vindication [the psalmists] are virtually asking for God's final judgement to be advanced in time.'[2] Finally, as we read these imprecatory psalms let us remain aware of our own sin and proneness to hypocrisy.

Psalm 35 falls into three main stanzas each one ending in a brief hymn of praise. In the first stanza (vv. 1–10), David begins by making his plea to God for his help (vv. 1–3). The military terminology may be only poetic but David prays that God will 'fight against those who fight against me' (v. 1). Then, in verses 4–6, David is more specific in his prayer for judgement on these people culminating in a prayer to 'let their way be dark and slippery, with the angel of the LORD pursuing them' (v. 6). The angel of the Lord appears in only two psalms—34 and 35. In Psalm 34 we were told that 'he encamps around those who fear him, and delivers them' (v. 7). Now here in Psalm 35, he is 'driving away' (v. 5) and 'pursuing' (v. 6) the enemies of God and of his people. As one commentator puts it, to God's people he brings salvation; to God's enemies he brings doom.[3] Or, as Alec Motyer more colourfully puts it: 'We met the angel in Psalm 34:7 where he was living in a mobile home so that he is always alongside, at the ready, to move when we move. Now we learn (Ps. 35:5–6) that he is active to chase and pursue.'[4] I don't think we need to concern ourselves too much with the speculation as to the identity of this angel. Sufficient for us is the promise that is ours in which God assures us, 'I will never leave you nor forsake you' (Heb. 13:5). That is why we can join with David in saying that despite all the trials of life that surround us: 'My soul will rejoice in the LORD, exulting in his salvation' (v. 9).

> **Sufficient for us is the promise that is ours in which God assures us, 'I will never leave you nor forsake you'.**

218

In the second stanza (vv. 11–18), David gives specifics of the 'fight' that he is enduring. Now we learn that those who are plotting and scheming against him are not only people he knows, but people to whom he has shown love and goodwill when they were going through the mill. Says David, 'they repay me evil for good' (v. 12) for when they were sick he had mourned and fasted, even prayed for them (v. 13). He'd treated them like bosom friends, like family (v. 14). But now David is the one who is struggling and in trouble, they're dancing in the streets (vv. 15–16). Derek Kidner suggests that it's as if the Good Samaritan of Jesus' parable himself later fell among thieves only to find that his former beneficiary was now his chief tormentor! And isn't this also a picture of us before we come to new life in Christ, that we ignore, insult, denigrate or mock the One who gave his very life for our salvation? For as the apostle Paul writes: 'But God shows his love for us in that while we were still sinners, Christ died for us' (Rom. 5:8). That truth alone should make us want to join with David in thankful praise: 'I will thank you in the great congregation; in the mighty throng I will praise you' (v. 18).

In the final stanza (vv. 19–28) we discover what maybe we'd thought was the case, that these turncoat friends have absolutely no reason to treat David in this way. These are those 'who hate ... without cause' (v. 19). They are purveyors of fake news—claiming to see what never happened (v. 21). What they fail to understand is the difference between their eyes and, as it were, God's eyes. They think they can get away with claims to see what never happened. The trouble for them is that God sees them seeing what never happened (v. 22)!

> They open wide their mouths against me;
> they say, "Aha, aha!
> Our eyes have seen it!"
> You have seen, O LORD; be not silent!
> O LORD, be not far from me!

Just as God told Moses that he had 'surely seen the affliction of my people who are in Egypt' (Ex. 3:7), so God today sees the affliction of his people and he also sees the actions of those who daily commit sin with impunity. We would all do well to adopt the prayer of the nineteenth century cleric and hymn writer Thomas Pollock (1836–96):

> We have not feared Thee as we ought,
> Nor heeded Thy all-seeing eye,
> Nor guarded word and deed and thought,
> Aware of One who stands nearby.
> Lord, give us faith to know Thee near
> And grant the grace of holy fear.[5]

To close the psalm, David invites us to 'shout for joy and be glad, and say evermore, "Great is the LORD, who delights in the welfare of his servants!"' (v. 27). And notice that word 'evermore'!

REFLECT ON THESE POINTS:

- We should remember that the Bible makes a clear distinction between those who are for God and those who are against him and the very different end awaiting them at a final judgement.
- 'But God shows his love for us in that while we were still sinners, Christ died for us' (Rom. 5:8). That truth alone should make us want to join with David in thankful praise.

PSALM 36

O love of God

We tend—mistakenly—to think of the love of God as a concept we meet only, or mainly, in the New Testament. Psalm 36 shows us how wrong we are! After an opening stanza concerned with the state of the arrogant wicked (vv. 1–4), David takes us to a higher plain as he wants to tell us about the 'steadfast love' of God, as well as his faithfulness, his righteousness and his justice (vv. 5–7a). He then uses a number of metaphors to illustrate God's love—the wings of a bird, a banquet, a river, a fountain and light (vv. 7b–9). And what a glorious love it is, this 'love divine, all loves excelling.' Finally, this leads to a prayer (vv. 10–12) that he might be preserved to enjoy God's love.

In the first stanza (vv. 1–4), it's as if David has been given godly insight into what makes the wicked tick. Put simply, it's that 'there is no fear of God before his eyes' (v. 1b). We've seen this before—in Psalms 2 and 14, for example. And for once, 'fear' relating to God doesn't mean reverence and awe, it means terror. They just don't take God seriously. In his book *In God We Doubt*, John Humphrys states that *if* God existed he would be 'exactly the sort of person you'd want your daughter to marry'!

And it's because they don't take God seriously that they can't see right from wrong (v. 2), they 'cease to act wisely' (v. 3) and walk in the wrong path (v. 4). More echoes of Psalm 14.

After all this, the second stanza (vv. 5–9) seems something of a *non sequitur*. But David now wants us to know about the God who must be, and indeed who deserves to be, taken seriously. And yet again we find the psalms to be a wonderful place for getting to know God—his character and his attributes. David presents four of God's attributes in these verses—his faithfulness (v. 5b), his righteousness (v. 6a) and his justice (v. 6b)—all bookended by his 'steadfast love' (vv. 5a, 7a).

When David talks of God's 'steadfast love' (vv. 5, 7, 10) he is using that Hebrew word *hesed* that we have come across before. In Psalm 13, we commented that whenever we read *hesed* we should always remember that it has overtones of amazing grace, whilst in Psalm 21, we quoted Dale Ralph Davis's vivid description of God's *hesed* love as 'love with super-glue on it.' This *hesed* love—loyal love—centres around what God has done for his people in that he has entered into a covenant with them, promising to do certain things for them and it reminds us that God is utterly faithful to this covenant commitment.[1] And David wants to tell us two things about God's covenant love—that it is both vast and precious. 'Your steadfast love, O LORD, extends to the heavens,' David writes (v. 5), before

223

exclaiming, 'How precious is your steadfast love, O God!' (v. 7). It was by his steadfast love that God promised to

It was by his steadfast love that God delivered his people out of Egypt.

make Abraham a mighty nation, blessing those who blessed him and cursing those who cursed him (Gen. 12:1–3). It was by his steadfast love that God delivered his people out of Egypt, bringing them through the Red Sea and the wilderness into the Land of Promise. And later, even in the midst of Babylonian exile, the prophet Jeremiah could write:

> The steadfast love of the LORD never ceases;
> his mercies never come to an end;
> they are new every morning;
> great is your faithfulness (Lam. 3:22–23).

And like Jeremiah, David in Psalm 36 links God's steadfast love with God's faithfulness: 'Your steadfast love, O LORD, extends to the heavens, your faithfulness to the clouds' (v. 5). And this is what God had always told his people: 'Know therefore that the LORD your God is God, the faithful God who keeps covenant and steadfast love with those who love him and keep his commandments' (Deut. 7:9). Arthur Pink writes on Psalm 37:5: 'Far above all finite comprehension is the unchanging faithfulness of God. Everything about God is great, vast, incomparable.

He never forgets, never fails, never falters, never forfeits his word.'[2] It always does our souls good to meditate upon the attributes of God and the psalms give us ample opportunity and encouragement.

But David has two other attributes of God to marvel at. God's righteousness, says the psalmist, 'is like the mountains of God' (v. 6), and mountains speak to us of permanence. I can still vividly remember taking a train journey from east to west across America. At one point, as we crossed Montana, the train snaked its way up to Marias Pass at 5,216 feet up in the Rockies. Such sights rightly instil in us feelings of awe and wonder. And so should the contemplation of the righteousness of God.

If God's righteousness is like the Marias Pass, his judgements are like the Mariana Trench.

But there is more, for David continues in the same verse, 'Your judgements are like the great deep.' The word rendered 'judgements' (or 'justice', NIV) is a judicial term referring not just to the judge's final judgement but to the whole of the court's record on a particular case. Derek Kidner therefore suggests that the reference could be to 'God's whole revealed will in Scripture.'[3] So if God's righteousness is like the Marias Pass, his judgements are like the Mariana Trench—at around 6.8 miles, the deepest part of earth's oceans!

In verse 7, David returns to God's steadfast, covenant love reminding us of how precious it is before giving us five metaphors to help us understand this boundless and unfailing love of God. But in a stunning contrast with verses 5–6, David moves 'from the immense to the intimate.'[4] We move from being awed by God's might and majesty to being 'honoured houseguests'[5]—offered spiritual shelter, food and drink (vv. 7–8) by our heavenly Father. And as always with God's spiritual provision for his people, it is abundant. We're offered not a snack or a meal, but an abundant feast (v. 8a)! We're offered not a glass of something, or a bottle, or even a crate, but a river (v. 8b)! As Jesus tells us: 'I came that they may have life and have it *abundantly*' (Jn. 10:10).

The metaphors continue in verse 9: 'For with you is the fountain of life; in your light do we see light.' And who can read this verse without thinking of their glorious fulfilment in the Lord Jesus Christ. Jesus tells the Samaritan woman at the well: 'Everyone who drinks of this water will be thirsty again, but whoever drinks of the water that I will give him will never be thirsty again. The water that I will give him will become in him a spring of water welling up to eternal life' (Jn. 4:13–14). And by this time John in his gospel has already named Jesus as 'the light of men' (Jn. 1:4) and will record Jesus saying,

'I am the light of the world' (Jn. 10:12). Let us join with David in his prayer that we might be kept by and in the love of God through all the perils of our earthly walk: 'Oh, continue your steadfast love to those who know you, and your righteousness to the upright in heart!' (v. 10).

> O love of God, our shield and stay
> Through all the perils of our way!
> Eternal love, in You we rest,
> Forever safe, forever blest.[6]

REFLECT ON THESE POINTS:

- David wants to tell us two things about God's covenant love—that it is both vast and precious.
- 'Far above all finite comprehension is the unchanging faithfulness of God. Everything about God is great, vast, incomparable. He never forgets, never fails, never falters, never forfeits his word.' (A.W. Pink)

PSALM 37

Cast your burden on the Lord

We come now to another of the Psalter's acrostic psalms—a kind of poetic way of saying that a particular subject is getting complete A to Z coverage.[1] And the subject is already a familiar one from previous psalms—the way of the wicked and the way of the righteous. But not just their way and their life, but the fruit of those lives and their final destinations. Acrostic psalms are best studied by themes rather than verse-by-verse. The psalm, written by David towards the end of his life (v. 25), is an exhortation not to fret nor be envious of the wicked. And the best way to stop us fretting and envying such folk is to think of what life produces and where life leads to for them compared with the fruit and final destiny of those who 'trust in the LORD' (v. 3).

First, then, what does the walk of wicked look like? Two characteristics stand out. First, they hate the godly (vv. 12, 14, 32). And the Bible has plenty of examples of the wicked hating godly people, plotting against them, lying in wait for them, even seeking to kill them. Think Potiphar's wife having Joseph imprisoned for a crime he refused to commit. Or of Queen Jezebel's oath to kill the prophet Elijah after the slaying of the prophets of Baal, or of Haman plotting to kill Mordecai in the book of Esther. Then in the New Testament there's the conspiracy to kill the apostle Paul in Acts 23. And of course, most supremely in the treatment and the death of the sinless, the righteous Lord Jesus Christ. 'The wicked lie in wait for the righteous, seeking their very lives,' says David. But not only do the wicked hate the godly, they are consumed with themselves (vv. 21, 35). They borrow but never repay—not because they can't but because they don't want to. After all, they think, 'borrowing' is a way to enrich myself. David thinks of these folk like laurel trees—that can grow to 18 metres high.

So, second, what is the 'fruit' of the wicked? In a word, they 'perish'—they're 'cut off' (vv. 9, 20, 22, 38). They think they're huge laurel trees, but in reality 'they fade like grass and wither like the green herb' (v. 2)—here today and gone tomorrow (v. 10). Think of someone like the great Emperor Julius Caesar who seemed for a time to dominate the known world and was adored, venerated and feared in all his earthly pomp and glory. But now, the name of Caesar is synonymous only with a slightly questionable form of salad, and a brand of cat food! How right the psalmist is:

> I have seen a wicked, ruthless man, spreading
>   himself like a green laurel tree.
> But he soon passed away, and behold, he was
>   no more;

though I sought him, he could not be found
(vv. 35–36).

And God's response to all this? 'But the LORD laughs at the wicked, for he sees that his day is coming' (v. 13)—'his day' being both the day he dies and the day of judgement. But we need to say that when David writes likes this, it's not in a sense of 'Yeah, right, they'll pay for that!' And we should avoid having such thoughts in our hearts as we read this psalm. Rather, David is admonishing us, he's warning us—that could be me, that could be you—literally, 'But for the grace of God . . .' And haven't you found it's what the Law of God so often does for us? It, as it were, holds up a mirror to us and condemns us, but thereby drives us outside of ourselves to a merciful and saving God. Yes, it shows us that we are wicked, that we will perish—but then tells us: 'For God so loved the world that he gave his only begotten Son, that whoever believes in him should *not* perish but have eternal life' (John 3:16, emphasis added).

'The righteous' are not 'perfect'—and they know it.

So what does the walk of the righteous look like? The first thing we need to understand is that 'the righteous' are not 'perfect'—and they know it. But they are those who are conscious of God's grace and forgiveness and thereby have been put right with God—and David is an obvious example of such. Three things characterise them. First, in contrast to the self-centredness of the wicked, the righteous have a God-given selflessness. 'The wicked borrows but does not pay back, but the righteous is generous and gives' (v. 21). Second, they have a God-given wisdom. 'The mouth of the righteous utters wisdom, and his tongue speaks justice.

> **If deliverance does not come this side of the grave, it will assuredly come on the other side.**

The law of his God is in his heart; his steps do not slip' (vv. 30–31). And third, they have a God-given protection—'He is their stronghold in time of trouble' (v. 39) and 'the LORD helps them and delivers them' (v. 40a). Why? 'Because they put their trust in him' (v. 40b). If deliverance does not come this side of the grave, it will assuredly come on the other side.

And that brings us finally to the fruit of the righteous. In 'the now', the Christian enjoys God's great provision (vv. 4, 16, 25), his faithfulness (v. 19), and his sovereignty—'The steps of a good man are ordered by the LORD and He delights in his way' (v. 23, NKJV). But as James Boice writes: 'It is not only [our] forward motion that is ordered by the Lord but also times of enforced inactivity. For the righteous, even these times have a gracious design.'[2] And in the 'not yet', the righteous will enjoy what David throughout refers to as an inheritance. And what a stark contrast this is with the bleak, one-dimensional 'fruit' of the wicked. So, we read that 'the evildoers will be cut off, but those who wait for the LORD shall inherit the land' (v. 9). And this can't just refer to the Promised Land. After all, they'd already inherited that. No. As one commentator explains: 'The "land" is throughout this psalm the promised possession—the land of God's presence, which is not merely a glorious past, but also a future rich in promises; and will finally become the inheritance of the true Israel.'[3]

And that's why the righteous are given numerous exhortations throughout this psalm. Not only are we cautioned against fretting and envy (v. 1), but also to 'trust in the LORD' (v. 3), 'delight in the LORD' (v. 4), 'commit your way to the LORD' (v. 5), 'rest in the LORD' (v. 7, KJV) and 'wait for the LORD' (v. 34). And of all those, I think I find the last is often the most difficult—the waiting. But it's always important to remember that whereas there are things of the finished work of Christ that are given to us now, mostly spiritual blessings in the work of the Holy Spirit in our hearts, many things are of the 'not yet'—blessings we will receive only at Christ's second coming, such as our resurrected bodies. In the meantime, as the apostle Paul writes, 'if we hope for what we do not see, we wait for it with patience' (Rom. 8:25). But for now, we do well to heed David's exhortation to 'commit your way to the LORD' (v. 5). The literal meaning here is to 'roll the burden of cares of your life's way upon God.'[4] It's the same thought that the apostle Peter has when he tells us to 'cast all your cares on him, because he cares for you' (1 Pet. 5:7). Have you done that?

> Cast your burden on the Lord,
> Only lean upon His Word;
> You will soon have cause to bless
> His eternal faithfulness.

> Jesus, guardian of Your flock,
> Be our stronghold and our rock!
> So when evil comes, we stand
> Shielded by Your powerful hand.[5]

REFLECT ON THESE POINTS:

- The Law of God, as it were, holds up a mirror to us and condemns us, but thereby drives us outside of ourselves to a merciful and saving God.
- The apostle Peter has when he tells us to 'cast all your cares on Him, because He cares for you' (1 Pet. 5:7). Have you done that?

PSALM 38

Salvation comes from God alone

Psalm 38 is one of the seven so-called penitential psalms but is probably the least known of all.[1] I doubt it's in your 'favourite psalms' list or that you've ever heard a sermon preached on it. And maybe that tells us something about our attitude to sin and penitence. In Archbishop Cranmer's *Book of Common Prayer* (1662), there is a confession of sin that includes these words: 'Mercifully forgive us our trespasses; receive and comfort us who are grieved and wearied with the burden of our sins.'[2] Are you, am I: 'grieved and wearied with the burden of our sins'? Or does such language seem somewhat over-the-top? If it does, then I suggest that we've lost sight of the holiness of God and the related fact that God hates sin—and not just sin in general, but our own, personal sin.

The psalm breaks into four parts. David begins by setting out his suffering (vv. 1–8) and he begins with his first prayer: 'O LORD, rebuke me not in your anger, nor discipline me in your wrath! (v. 1). We read something very similar from David at the beginning of Psalm 6. I think there are two points we need to learn from this. First, human suffering is not always a sign of God's displeasure. That's surely what we're meant to learn from the book of Job. And elsewhere, Scripture tells us that 'As many as I *love*, I rebuke and chasten' (Rev. 3:19, KJV). Second, if God punished our sin in his wrath according to our deserving, none of us would survive on this earth a moment longer, and Scripture echoes that truth too. Jeremiah prays: 'Correct me, O LORD, but in justice: not in your anger, lest you bring me to nothing' (Jer. 10:24). And in another psalm we read this question put to God: 'If you, O LORD, should mark iniquities, O LORD, who could stand?' (Ps. 130:3). And the implied answer is 'no-one!'

Then in the second section, we read of David's response to his great suffering—his longing and sighing (v. 9), his weakness (v. 10) and his loneliness (v. 11). And here we also find an instructive contrast between the fickleness of man and the faithfulness of God. Whilst David goes through the mill, his friends and companions 'stand aloof'; even his family 'stand far off' (v. 11). One is reminded of the apostle Paul imprisoned in Rome and writing to Timothy: 'At my first defence no one came to stand by me, but all deserted me' (2 Tim. 4:16). But what do we read next from the apostle's pen? 'But'—I do love these biblical 'buts'—'But the LORD stood by me and strengthened me' (v. 17). And the psalmist's experience is the same, for we read that David is confident that when it comes to God: 'All my longing is before you; my sighing is not hidden from you' (Ps. 38:9). This is *El Roi*—the God who sees me (Gen. 16.14). What a comfort is God's all-seeing eye to the believer.

In the psalm's third section we find David confessing his

sin: 'I confess my iniquity; I am sorry for my sin' (v. 18). But we do need to be careful here for as Charles Spurgeon rightly remarks on this verse: 'To be sorry for sin is no atonement for it.'[3] The words 'I have sinned' passed the lips of both Pharaoh (Ex. 10:16) and King Saul (1. Sam. 15:30), but Scripture nowhere records that

'To be sorry for sin is no atonement for it.'

either received God's forgiveness. But, as Spurgeon goes on to say, being sorry is the first step in receiving forgiveness. Think, if you will, of the prodigal son in Jesus' parable in Luke 15. In verses 11–16, he is sinning. But by verse 17 he is sorry for his sin. He even says as much—to himself—in verses 18–19. But it's not until verse 21 that he confesses his sin to his father and seeks—and receives—forgiveness. As John Stott perceptively puts it: 'he had to "come to himself" before he could "come to his father."'[4]

In this section of the psalm we also find that David is heeding one of the exhortations we read in Psalm 37—'Rest in the LORD and *wait patiently* for him' (v. 7, NKJV). Here in Psalm 38 at verse 15, David tells us: 'But for you, O LORD, do I wait; it is you, O Lord my God, who will answer,' a verse which in the Hebrew text has three of the Old Testament names for God—Jehovah (LORD), Adonai (Lord) and Elohim (God).[5] How wonderful the psalms are in reminding us of who God is through the majesty of his names. So here we have God as the I am who I am (Ex. 3:14), the Sovereign

Lord (Gen. 15:1) and the Creator God (Gen. 1:1). Such a God is worthy of our waiting. His timing is always right: never too soon and never too late as he works his sovereign will in our lives. The truths of this verse (15) are echoed in one of Charles Wesley's lesser-known hymns:

> Jesus, my strength, my hope,
> On Thee I cast my care;
> With humble confidence look up,
> And know Thou hearest prayer.
> Give me on Thee to wait
> Till I can all things do;
> On Thee, almighty to create,
> Almighty to renew.[6]

Each of the psalm's four stanzas is introduced by the word 'LORD' and we find the last in verse 21 introducing David's concluding three-fold prayer: 'Do not forsake me, O LORD! O my God, be not far from me! Make haste to help me, O LORD, my salvation!' (vv. 21–22). Calvin commenting on these two verses writes: 'David briefly states the chief point which he desired, and the sum of his whole prayer; namely, that whereas he was forsaken of men, and grievously afflicted, God would receive him and raise him up again.'[7] But David has come a long way in these twenty-two verses. The God who at the psalm's beginning was the source of David's rebuke for sin is now both his Lord and his salvation. That's what spending time meditating on God and his Word can do for your soul! David is reminding us of the comparative inadequacy of human power to save—that God is the only trustworthy source of deliverance and salvation. And as he will tell us later in Psalm 60: 'Vain is the salvation of man!' (v. 11b)—or literally 'human salvation is worthless!' That's why the apostle Paul reminds us: 'For by grace you have been saved through faith. And this is not your own doing; it is the gift of God, not a result of works, so that no one may boast' (Eph. 2:8–9).

> Salvation comes from God alone
> Which we can never win;
> Your love revealed on Calvary
> Is cleansing for our sin.
>
> On earth we long for heaven's joy
> Where, bowed before Your throne,
> We know You, Father, Spirit, Son,
> As God, and God alone.[8]

REFLECT ON THESE POINTS:

- What a comfort is God's all-seeing eye to the believer.
- How wonderful the psalms are in reminding us of who God is through the majesty of his names.
- God's timing is always right: never too soon and never too late as he works his sovereign will in our lives.

PSALM 39

From grace to glory

Psalm 39 has two inter-related themes: the fleeting nature, or vanity, of our lives, and the God-separating effects of our sin. Neither of these are easy matters to address honestly and realistically. Maybe that's why Psalm 39 is another of those psalms which is rarely read or preached in our churches. Indeed, David admits in the opening stanza (vv. 1–3) that these are profoundly difficult matters to verbalise. And because he doesn't want to give a bad witness to unbelievers, David has 'guarded [his] mouth with a muzzle, so long as the wicked are in [his] presence' (v. 1). But as many of us discover from painful experience, not talking about the things we need to talk about is 'to no avail' and 'my distress grew worse' (v. 2).

In his devotional commentary on this psalm, Alec Motyer draws attention to the two extremes to which Christians often go in talking of matters relating to the fleeting nature of life and of imminent death. 'We have all heard Christians speak in such a carelessly confident way about dying that their testimony sounded glib and brash, failing to take into account the solemnity of death, or that in the majority of cases it comes as an unwelcome intruder into a life we are loathe to leave.'[1] On the other hand, we have maybe heard Christians speak as if death was the very worst thing that could happen to them, or other believers.

But by the second stanza (vv. 4–6), David has overcome his enforced silence and speaks to God. And although it's not at all obvious in most of our English translations, the word rendered 'a mere breath' at the end of verses 5 and 11 is the same Hebrew word that we find used constantly by Solomon in Ecclesiastes and is in most translations rendered as 'vanity':

> Vanity of vanities, says the Preacher,
> vanity of vanities! All is vanity (Ecc. 1:2).

David is wanting us to see the utter transience of human life. David is wanting us to see the utter transience of human life. It's a New Testament theme too where we read: 'What is your life? For you are a mist that appears for a little time and then vanishes' (Jas. 4:14). Comments Franz Delitzsch: 'The duration of human life is as a vanishing nothing before God the eternal One.'[2] Hence David's prayer in verse 4 that he may know 'the measure of my days; let me know how fleeting I am!' It is what Moses prays for in Psalm 90: 'So teach us to number our days that we may get a heart of wisdom' (v. 12). That's what the wise and godly person prays, whereas 'mankind' merely 'heaps up wealth and does not know who will gather [it]' (Ps. 39:6). As the saying goes, 'Have you ever seen a hearse with a trailer?' And what does God say to the one who thinks life is only about money and 'stuff'? 'You fool, this night your soul is required of you, and the things you have prepared, whose will they be?' (Lk. 12:20).

In the third stanza (vv. 7–11) we find David being disciplined for his 'transgressions' (v. 8) and his 'sin' (v. 10). This raises the question: 'Why does God do this to his own people?' We've already been reminded how frail and fleeting our life is anyway, but why does God seem to add to its weaknesses? It's the same question that Job raises:

> What is man, that you make so much of him,
> and that you set your heart on him,
> visit him every morning
> and test him every moment? . . .
> If I sin, what do I do to you, you watcher of
> mankind?
> Why have you made me your mark?
> Why have I become a burden to you?
> Why do you not pardon my transgression
> and take away my iniquity?
> For now I shall lie in the earth;
> you will seek me, but I shall not be (Job 7:17–21).

Christopher Ash comments how these thoughts parody and turn upside down the wonderfully positive theology we find David expressing in Psalm 8.[3] In that psalm David asks, 'What is man?' and finds that God graciously clothes him with dignity and responsibility for the world—a truly wonderful truth. But here in Psalm 39—like Job of old—David is asking, 'What is man that God bothers with me? Why doesn't God just forget about me and leave me alone?'[4] The answer is what James Boice calls 'the paradox of human existence.'[5] Yes, we may be, as Shakespeare memorably put it, 'but a walking shadow, a poor player that struts and frets his hour upon the stage, and then is heard no more.'[6] But we are so much more than that, for though our life is brief here on earth, we are of eternal value to God. And that is why he disciplines us, for 'those whom I love, I reprove and discipline' (Rev. 3:19).

And the hope of eternity takes us into the psalm's final stanza (vv. 12–13). David by now realises that, here on earth, he is merely 'a sojourner' and 'a guest, like all my fathers' (v. 12)—or as the NIV has it, 'an alien' and 'a stranger.' These terms are of great biblical significance. First, this is how Abraham (Gen. 23:4) and Moses (Ex. 2:22) described themselves whilst living respectively in Canaan and Egypt. Second, these were the terms also used to describe foreign residents in Israel who were to be well-treated. 'You shall treat the stranger who sojourns with you as the native among you, and you shall love him as yourself, for you were strangers in the land of Egypt: I am the LORD your God' (Lev. 19:34).

But, of course, these names have New Testament connotations as well: 'Beloved, I urge you as sojourners and exiles to abstain from the passions of the flesh, which wage war against your soul' (1 Pet. 2:11). And so we are exhorted to see ourselves living in this world as pilgrims—as 'strangers and exiles on the earth' as those who 'make it clear that they are seeking a homeland' and 'desire a better country, that is, a heavenly one' (Heb. 11:13–16). In David's final plea (v. 13) we see just how honest Scripture is, for who among us hasn't thought this or something similar in one of our low moments? We also glimpse God's compassion for us in such times and that, as David will write in a later psalm: God 'knows our frame; he remembers that we are dust' (Ps. 103:14). In the meantime, let us lift our pilgrim eyes to our sure and steadfast hope of heavenly rest and joy:

We are exhorted to see ourselves living in this world as pilgrims—as 'strangers and exiles on the earth'.

> Onward, then, from grace to glory,
> Armed by faith and spurred by prayer;
> Heaven's eternal day before me;
> God's own hand shall guide me there.

Soon shall close my earthly mission,
Swiftly pass my pilgrim days,
Hope soon change to glad fruition,
Faith to sight, and prayer to praise.[7]

REFLECT ON THESE POINTS:

- 'The duration of human life is as a vanishing nothing before God the eternal One.' (Franz Delitzsch)
- But though our life is brief here on earth, we are of eternal value to God.
- Let us lift our pilgrim eyes to our sure and steadfast hope of heavenly rest and joy.

Psalm 40

A sacrifice of nobler name

One of the rewards of reading through the psalms consecutively is that we get to see how themes are developed over a number of psalms. A theme of Psalms 37–39 has been that of waiting for God. 'Wait for the Lord and keep his way,' David instructed us at Psalm 37:34. Then in Psalm 38, he prayed to God telling him, 'But for you, O Lord, do I wait' (v. 15). David was still waiting in Psalm 39: 'And now, O Lord, for what do I wait? My hope is in you' (v. 7). And that's the backdrop against which we should read in the opening verse of Psalm 40: 'I waited patiently for the Lord; he inclined to me and heard my cry.' Waiting was rewarded. Indeed, our English translations are rather prosaic in saying that David 'waited patiently.' The New English Bible gets closer to the original with, 'I waited, waited for the Lord.' Furthermore, God not only '*inclined* to me' (ESV) but 'he *bent down* to me and heard my cry' (NEB) conjuring up the picture of a loving father bending down to hear and comfort his distressed child. As David will tell us in a later psalm: 'As a father shows compassion to his children, so the Lord shows compassion to those who fear him' (Ps. 103:13).

And God is not only a God who shows compassion but

he rescues too—'from the pit of destruction' (v. 2). James Boice surmises that for David this might relate to the Bathsheba and Uriah incident of 2 Samuel 11. But for us, Boice says that this could be a pit of besetting sin, of bad habits or of severe circumstances.[1] But notice how David is not self-obsessed, even in the midst of such trials. No! His thoughts and his voice

Notice how David is not self-obsessed, even in the midst of such trials.

rise in praise to God: 'He put a new song in my mouth; a song of praise to our God' (v. 3a). And he wants others to be blessed by his blessing: 'Many will see and fear, and put their trust in the LORD' (v. 3b). Are we as God-centred and others-centred at times of trial and distress?

Then in the second stanza (vv. 4–5), David sings of the blessedness of those who put their trust in God rather than resorting to the sins of pride and dishonesty (v. 4)—more echoes of Psalm 1. And he praises God for his 'wondrous deeds' and his 'thoughts towards us' (v. 5), all making God incomparable. In one of the loveliest chapters in Isaiah, chapter 40—the one that begins, 'Comfort ye, comfort ye my people, saith your God'—Isaiah asks the people rhetorically: 'To whom will you liken God, or what likeness compare with him?' (Is. 40:18). And a few verses later, God asks the same question: '"To whom then will you compare me, that I should be like him?" says the Holy

One' (Is. 40:25). And the implied answer to both questions is 'no one, nothing!'

This brings us to the heart of the psalm—the third stanza, verses 6–8, which is quoted by the writer to the Hebrews in the New Testament who puts these words, as it were, into the mouth of Christ (Heb. 10:5–7). And this provides us an opportunity to say something about how the psalms point towards the Lord Jesus Christ. Now there are those who try to find the Messiah behind every bush (burning, or otherwise) in the Old Testament! And we do need to beware of falling into extremes. At one extreme we see the psalms merely as beautiful poems that speak about life centuries before Christ from which we can draw spiritual wisdom and comfort. At the other, we talk about psalms being 'Messianic' and try to force into Jesus' mouth words that he never would have said. And so here, the trouble with describing Psalm 40 as 'Messianic' is that we're clearly going to get into difficulties later on when in verse 12 we read that 'my iniquities have overtaken me .. . they are more than the hairs of my head.' What we need to see is that David is, however, able to write in a way that is both true of himself and yet also prophetically points forward to Christ. And that's what we have in verses 6–8. These verses have two perspectives: a David perspective and a Messianic perspective.

What David is doing in these verses from his perspective is reminding us of the important biblical principle that with God obedience always takes preference over sacrifice. Indeed, it was this very principle that led to God's rejection of King Saul and the crown passing to David. Saul had been told by God to strike the Amalekites and to destroy everything. But Saul and his men 'took of the spoil, sheep and oxen . . .' in order that they might, as the King told Samuel, 'sacrifice to the LORD your God' (1 Sam. 15:21). And Samuel's response? 'Has the LORD as great delight in burnt offerings and sacrifices, as in obeying the voice of the LORD? Behold, to obey is better than sacrifice, and to listen than the fat of rams' (1 Sam. 15:22).[2]

But what David is also doing is what we saw him do in Psalm 22. He is, as the apostle Peter says of David regarding another psalm, 'Being therefore a prophet . . . [David] foresaw and spoke of . . . the Christ' (Acts 2:30–31). Thus these verses also have a Messianic perspective, especially in verses 7 and 8. For only Christ could *truly* say that 'in the scroll of the book [that is the Scriptures] it is written of me: I delight to do your will, O my God; your law is within my heart.' And the best way to understand the Messianic implications of these verses is to see the context in which the writer to the Hebrews sets them. He's just told us that the old sacrificial law was 'but a shadow of the good things to come' (Heb. 10:1). Why only a shadow? 'For it is impossible for the blood of bulls and goats to take away sins' (Heb. 10:4). 'Consequently,' he continues, 'when Christ came into the world, he said . . .' and quotes Psalm 40:6–8. The blood of bulls and goats couldn't take away sins but merely pointed forward to the One who could, and did—on the cross at Calvary. 'To obey is better than sacrifice,' Samuel had said. But who had ever obeyed like Jesus? As Richard Phillips puts it: 'Who had ever perfectly fulfilled the Father's will, both in terms of the moral law and in terms of the work he was given to do?'[3] 'I have come to do your will, O God' (Heb. 10:7).

And our response? To trust in God's only availing sacrifice for sin—the Lord Jesus Christ—and then seek, in the power of the Holy Spirit, to live a life of God-glorifying obedience. Then tell others the good news so that we can say with David: 'I have not concealed your steadfast love and your faithfulness from the great congregation' (v. 10).

> For all the blood of beasts
> On Jewish altars slain
> Could never give the conscience peace
> Or wash away its stain:
>
> But Christ, the heavenly Lamb,
> Takes all our sins away—
> A sacrifice of nobler name
> And richer blood than they.[4]

REFLECT ON THESE POINTS:

- God not only 'inclined to me' but 'he bent down to

me and heard my cry' conjuring up the picture of a loving father bending down to hear and comfort his distressed child.

- Are we as God-centred and others-centred as David at times of trial and distress?
- Our response should be to trust in God's only availing sacrifice for sin—the Lord Jesus Christ—and then seek, in the power of the Holy Spirit, to live a life of God-glorifying obedience.

PSALM 41

Betrayal and blessing

Psalm 41 is the last psalm in Book I of the Psalter. It seems likely that all these forty-one psalms were written by David. He is, after all, the stated author of thirty-seven of them, and it is likely he also wrote the other four—Psalms 1, 2, 10 and 33. The next David psalm is not until number 51. Psalm 41's position may well account for its first and last verses. Book I began with a beatitude—'Blessed is the man who walks not in the counsel of the wicked' (Ps. 1:2), and Psalm 41, too, begins in the same way—'Blessed is the one who considers the poor' (Ps. 41:1). Its final verse is a doxology and the final verse of the concluding psalms of the remaining four books also end with a doxology—Psalm 72:20 (Book II, Psalm 89:52 (Book III) and Psalm 106:48 (Book IV), whilst the whole of the final psalm—150—is given over to a six-verse doxology!

Setting the doxology aside for the moment, the remaining twelve verses of Psalm 41 divide into three parts. In the opening three verses we find an echo of another of our Lord's beatitudes. Just as Psalm 37 is the Psalter's version of the third beatitude—'Blessed are the meek, for they shall inherit the earth' (Matt. 5:5)—these opening verses of Psalm 41 are the Psalter's version of the fifth beatitude—'Blessed are the merciful, for they shall receive mercy' (Matt. 5:7)—for they contain the promise that 'the one who considers the poor' will be blessed and delivered (v. 1), protected and kept alive (v. 2), sustained and restored (v. 3). By 'the poor' is meant not so much those who lack money but those who are weak, helpless and at a low ebb.[1] And to 'consider' them implies 'giving careful thought to this person's situation, rather than perfunctory help.'[2] Reading this with Christian eyes, we would do well to see this as a signpost to our Lord's teaching in the Olivet Discourse:

> Then the King will say to those on his right, 'Come, you who are blessed by my Father, inherit the kingdom prepared for you from the foundation of the world. For I was thirsty and you gave me drink, I was a stranger and you welcomed me, I was naked and you clothed me, I was sick and you visited me, I was in prison and you came to me' (Matt. 25:34–36).

But let us be clear, these are not good works done in the hope of salvation, or even of any kind of heavenly reward. Rather, 'these deeds reveal who they already are— the elect of God, the people saved from their sins by the redemptive sacrifice of God's Son.'[3]

But then in verses 4–10, we discover that David is suffering from at least three afflictions—a guilty conscience (v. 4), a serious illness (v. 5) and a betrayal by a close friend (v. 9). First, David conscious of sin, prays that God might 'be gracious' to him (ESV) or 'have mercy' on him (NIV). Indeed, this is the same Hebrew word with which David will open Psalm 51—'Have mercy on me, O God.' We have noticed before David's commendably down to earth view of sin. He doesn't dress it up with fancy language. He calls it for what it is, and most important, he knows that sin is always sin against God (v. 4). It's also worth noting that the healing for which David prays in this verse is healing of the soul, not of the body. 'Heal *my soul*,' David prays, 'for I have sinned against you' (NKJV). This raises the question as to whether or not we take the same view of sin—that it's an affront to the holiness and righteousness of God and requires spiritual healing by God alone? Or do we try to sweep it under the rug or dress it up with fancy euphemisms?

Do we try to sweep sin under the rug or dress it up with fancy euphemisms?

Second, David is clearly in a bad way physically. Scripture makes no record of any serious illness in David's life, but that does not take away the authenticity of David's descriptions in this psalm or in others such as Psalms 6 and 38. David's enemies are having a field day at David's expense. They're running a countdown clock to his demise (v. 5) and rather than wishing him well, these folk wish him unwell (v. 7). Their whispering campaign would be hard to bear at the best of times, but serious ill-health just exacerbates the problem.

But then we discover David's third problem. For the whisperers and ill-wishers are not just the usual suspects, but 'even my close friend in whom I trusted, who ate my bread, has lifted his heel against me' (v. 9). 'Et tu, Brute?' as Julius Caesar famously asked, showing the shock of being betrayed by a close friend. David does not reveal who this person is, but most commentators suggest that the biblical evidence would point to it being Ahithophel, David's trusted friend and adviser, who joined the rebel forces of Absalom when Absalom, David's son, led a conspiracy against his father. David had sorrow added upon sorrow to discover that such a close friend and counsellor was now advising Absalom. Hence David's prayer which God answered, not by turning Ahithophel's advice to foolishness but by causing Absalom to reject it! We then read that 'when Ahithophel saw that his counsel was not followed . . . he set his house in order and hanged himself' (2 Sam. 17:23).

And that narrative leads us to the circumstances that part of Psalm 41:9 is quoted by Jesus in the New Testament. The setting is the Last Supper and Jesus' foretelling of Judas' betrayal of him. Says Jesus: 'But the Scripture will be fulfilled, "He who ate my bread has lifted his heel against me"' (Jn. 13:18). Notice that our Lord quotes only the second half of David's verse, omitting the reference to 'my close friend in whom I trusted.' After all, Jesus himself 'knew what was in man' (Jn. 2:25). He always knew what Judas would do, that he was never 'a close friend' and not one to be trusted. But when we feel let down, even betrayed, by close friends or family, we can know that Jesus has experienced this in the most extreme way possible. Scripture also warns us of the fate of those who betray God's chosen ones. I think we are meant to notice the similar fates of Ahithophel and Judas.[4]

But David returns to praise God in the closing verses of Psalm 41. And as we have seen so often, what motivates him— and should motivate us—is the remembrance of who God is, what God has done, and what God promises to do for us. 'By this I know that you delight in me . . . you have upheld me because of my integrity, and set me in your presence forever' (vv. 11–12). If we are truly in Christ, then like David ours is an eternal inheritance in the presence of God. As John Newton puts it:

Scripture warns us of the fate of those who betray God's chosen ones.

> Solid joys and lasting treasure,
> None but Zion's children know.[5]

Therefore, we join with David in his closing doxology:

> Blessed be the LORD, the God of Israel,

from everlasting to everlasting!
Amen and Amen (v. 13).

REFLECT ON THESE POINTS:

- Our 'good works' are not done in the hope of salvation, or even of any kind of heavenly reward. Rather, 'these deeds reveal who they already are—the elect of God, the people saved from their sins by the redemptive sacrifice of God's Son.' (Knox Chamblin)
- And as we have seen so often, what motivates David to praise God—and should motivate us—is the remembrance of who God is, what God has done, and what he promises to do for us.

ENDNOTES

Psalm 1

1   Derek Kidner, *Psalms 1–72* (Downers Grove, IL: Inter-Varsity Press, 2008), pp. 64–65.

2   In the Hebrew *ish* is used for a representative example and does not relate to gender.

3   Dale Ralph Davis, *The Way of the Righteous in the Muck of Life* (Fearn, Ross-shire: Christian Focus, 2016), p. 15.

4   Ibid. p. 19.

Psalm 2

1   This opening paragraph is drawn from a sermon preached by David Turner on 27 April 2014 at All Souls Church, Langham Place, London.

2   Quoted in James Montgomery Boice, *Psalms 1–41: An Expositional Commentary* (Grand Rapids, MI: Baker Books, 1994), p. 24.

3   David Gooding, *An Unshakeable Kingdom: The Letter to the Hebrews for Today* (Coleraine: Myrtlefield House, 2013), p. 43.

4   James Johnston, *The Psalms: Volume 1–Psalms 1 to 41* (Wheaton, IL: Crossway, 2015) p. 38.

5   Charles Wesley, 'Rejoice, the Lord is King' (1746).

Psalm 3

1   Iain M. Duguid, *Living in the Gap between Promise and Reality: The Gospel According to Abraham* (Phillipsburg, NJ: P&R Publishing, 1999), p. 1.

2   The outline for this chapter is in part suggested by Dale Ralph Davis, *The Way of the Righteous in the Muck of Life: Psalms 1–12* (Fearn, Ross-shire: Christian Focus, 2016), pp. 39–48.

3   Arthur W. Pink, *The Attributes of God* (Grand Rapids, MI: Baker Books, 1975), p. 7.

4   Davis, *The Way of the Righteous in the Muck of Life: Psalms 1–12*, pp. 41–44.

5   Joseph Hart, 'How good is the God we adore' (1759).

6   Alec Motyer, *Treasures of the King: Psalms from the life of David* (Nottingham: Inter-Varsity Press, 2007), p. 140.

7   Adrian Howard and Pat Turner, 'Salvation belongs to our God' © 1985 Restoration Music.

Psalm 4

1   David Broder, *The Pursuit of the Presidency 1980* (New York: G. P. Putnam, 1980), p. 313.

2   James Johnston, *The Psalms: Volume 1–Psalms 1 to 41* (Wheaton, IL: Crossway, 2015), p. 61.

3   George Beverly Shea, 'I'd rather have Jesus' (1922).

4   William Romanis, 'Round me falls the night' (1878).

Psalm 5

1   James Johnston, *The Psalms: Volume 1–Psalms 1–41* (Wheaton, IL: Crossway, 2015), p. 63.

2   William A. VanGemeren, *Psalms: The Expositor's Bible Commentary* (Grand Rapids, MI: Zondervan, 2008), Vol. 5, p. 116, quoted in Johnston, The Psalms, p. 66.

3   Dale Ralph Davis, *The Way of the Righteous in the Muck of Life: Psalms 1–12* (Fearn, Ross-shire: Christian Focus, 2016), p. 66.

4   Charlotte Elliott (1834).

Psalm 6

1   Charles H. Spurgeon, *The Treasury of David* (Peabody, MA: Hendrickson, 2016), Vol. 1, p. 57.

2   Psalms 6, 13, 35, 74, 79, 80, 89, 90, 94 and 119.

3   Samuel J. Stone, 'The church's one foundation' (1866).

4   I am grateful to Gerald H. Wilson, *Psalms Volume 1: The NIV Application Commentary* (Grand Rapids, MI: Zondervan, 2002), pp. 185–86 for the thoughts in this paragraph.

5 See Mark 12:26–27 where Jesus quotes Exodus 3:6.

6 Gerald H. Wilson, *Psalms Volume 1*, p. 180.

7 Dale Ralph Davis, *The Way of the Righteous in the Muck of Life* (Fearn, Ross-shire: Christian Focus, 2016), p. 77.

8 Charles H. Spurgeon, *The Treasury of David*, p. 57.

9 John Newton, 'Amazing grace! how sweet the sound' (1779).

Psalm 7

1 *The Guardian*, 1 October 1969, p.1.

2 In Act III Scene II of *Hamlet*, Queen Gertrude has the line, 'The lady doth protest too much, methinks.'

3 Joseph M. Scriven, 'What a friend we have in Jesus' (1855).

4 Alec Motyer, *Treasures of the King* (Nottingham: Inter-Varsity Press, 2007), p. 18.

5 Jonathan Allen and Amie Parnes, *Shattered: Inside Hillary Clinton's Doomed Campaign* (New York: Crown, 2017), p. 285.

6 James Russell Lowell, *The Present Crisis* (1841).

7 Joseph M. Scriven.

Psalm 8

1 Quoted in James Montgomery Boice, *Psalms: An Expositional Commentary* (Grand Rapids, MI: Baker Books, 1994), Vol. 1, p. 67.

2 Gerald H. Wilson, *Psalms: The NIV Application Commentary* (Grand Rapids, MI: Zondervan, 2002), Vol. 1, p. 200.

3 James Montgomery Boice, *Psalms: An Expositional Commentary* (Grand Rapids, MI: Baker Books, 1994), Vol. 1, p. 69.

4 J.J. Stewart Perowne, *The Book of Psalms* (Grand Rapids, MI: Zondervan, 1976), p. 156.

5 James Johnston, *The Psalms: Volume 1 – Psalm 1–41* (Wheaton, IL: Crossway, 2015), pp. 100–101.

6 Carl Gustav Boberg translated by Stuart K. Hine, 'O Lord my God' (1949).

Psalm 9

1   James Johnston, *The Psalms Volume 1* (Wheaton, IL: Crossway, 2015), p. 112.
2   Jonas Myrin and Matt Redman, 'Bless the Lord, O my soul' (© 2011 Thankyou Music)
3   Anthony J. Bennett, *US Government and Politics 2018* (Banbury: Hodder Education, 2018), p. 60.
4   *Westminster Shorter Catechism* (1647).
5   David G. Preston, *Praise!* website at www.praise.org.uk accessed 19 March 2020.
6   Gerald H. Wilson, *The NIV Application Commentary: Psalms* (Grand Rapids, MI: Zondervan, 2002), Vol. 1, p. 229.
7   Charles H. Spurgeon, *The Treasury of David* (Peabody, MA: Hendrickson, 2016), Vol. 1, p. 101.
8   David G. Preston, 'The Lord is king' (c. 1983).

Psalm 10

1   Gerald H. Wilson, *The NIV Application Commentary: Psalms Volume 1* (Grand Rapids, MI: Zondervan, 2002), p. 235.
2   P. C. Craigie quoted in James Montgomery Boice, *Psalms: An Expositional Commentary* (Grand Rapids, MI: Baker Books, 1994), Vol. 1, p. 84.
3   Samuel J. Stone, 'The church's one foundation' (1866).

Psalm 11

1   'Bishop Cottrell Urges Inclusion', *Church Times*, 17 March 2017. Accessed online 9 April 2020.
2   I am grateful for this helpful outline to James Montgomery Boice, *Psalms: An Expositional Commentary* (Grand Rapids, MI: Baker Books, 1994), Vol. 1.
3   'In God will I trust', The Psalter 1912.
4   See, for example, Psalm 18:6; Psalm 29:9.

5 Charles Spurgeon, *The Treasury of David* (Peabody, MA: Hendrickson, 2016), Vol. 1, p. 130.

6 Edith Margaret Clarkson, 'Let not your hearts be troubled' (1962).

Psalm 12

1 Derek Kidner, *Psalms 1–72* (Downers Grove, IL: Inter-Varsity Press, 2008), p. 91.

2 Martin Luther, 'Ach Gott von Himmel, sieh darein' (1524), translated by George Macdonald (1876).

3 Gerald H. Wilson, *The NIV Application Commentary: Psalms* (Grand Rapids, MI: Zondervan, 2002), Vol. 1, p. 269.

4 James Edmeston, 'Lead us, heavenly Father, lead us' (1821).

Psalm 13

1 John Risbridger, *The Message of Worship* (Nottingham: Inter-Varsity Press, 2015), p. 253.

2 Respectively Genesis 4:9; Genesis 18:23; Exodus 3:13.

3 James Montgomery Boice, *Psalms: An Expositional Commentary* (Grand Rapids, MI: Baker Books, 1994), Vol. 1, p. 108.

4 Joseph M. Scriven, 'What a friend we have in Jesus' (1855).

5 Different translations use different words: 'unfailing love' (NIV); 'lovingkindness' (NASB); 'mercy' (KJV, NKJV).

6 Dale Ralph Davis, *Slogging Along in the Paths of Righteousness* (Fearn, Ross-shire: Christian Focus, 2014), p. 21.

7 George Matheson, 'O love that wilt not let me go' (1882).

Psalm 14

1 Derek Kidner, *Psalms 1–72* (Downers Grove, IL: InterVarsity Press, 2008), p. 95.

2 James Montgomery Boice, *Romans: An Expository Commentary* (Grand Rapids, MI: Baker Books, 1991), Vol. 1, p. 293.

3 Ibid. p. 295.

4 Henry W. Baker, 'The King of love my Shepherd is' (1868).

5 Martin Luther, 'Ach Gott vom Himmel, sieh darein' (1524), translated by George Macdonald (1876).

Psalm 15

1 In Myles Coverdale's 1535 translation of the Bible, Psalm 15 is divided into seven verses – verse 4 being divided into two, and the last line of verse 5 forming a separate verse (v. 7). This is the translation which survives today in the 1662 *Book of Common Prayer* in some Anglican churches.

2 John Stott, *Favourite Psalms: Growing Closer to God* (Mill Hill: Monarch, 2003), p. 13.

3 Joseph Conrad, *Lord Jim* (1900), chapter 34.

4 James Johnston, *The Psalms* (Wheaton, IL: Crossway, 2015), Vol. 1, p. 169.

5 John Stott, *Favourite Psalms,* p. 13.

6 William Dunn Longstaff, 'Take time to be holy' (c. 1882).

Psalm 16

1 Henry Blunt, *A Family Exposition of the Pentateuch* (London: Hatchard, 1851), Vol. 3, p. 29.

2 Frances Jane Van Alstyne, 'Blessed assurance, Jesus is mine' (1873).

Psalm 17

1 Allan Harman, *Psalms* (Fearn, Ross-shire: Christian Focus, 2011), Vol. 1, p. 180.

2 J. J. Stewart Perowne, *The Book of Psalms* (Grand Rapids, MI: Zondervan, 1976), p. 204.

3 Joseph M. Scriven, 'What a friend we have in Jesus' (1855).

4 Allan Harman, *Psalms*, Vol. 1, p. 183.

5 Ebenezer A. Tydeman, 'I have a Friend whose faithful love.' No date is given to the composition of this hymn. Tydeman, born in 1842, ended his days as pastor of Godalming Baptist Church, Surrey. He died there in 1914.

Psalm 18

1 Alec Motyer, *Treasures of the King: Psalms from the life of David* (Nottingham: Inter-Varsity Press, 2007), p. 85.
2 Ibid, p. 87.
3 James Montgomery Boice, *Psalms: An Expository Commentary* (Grand Rapids, MI: Baker Books, 1994), Vol. 1, p. 150.
4 Michael Wilcock, *The Message of Psalms 1–72* (Nottingham: Inter-Varsity Press, 2001), p. 65.
5 Respectively Exodus 15:2; Deuteronomy 32:15; 1 Samuel 2:1; Psalm 18:46; Luke 1:47.
6 James Montgomery Boice, *Foundations of the Christian Faith* (Downers Grove, IL: Inter-Varsity Press, 1986), p. 256.
7 Timothy Dudley Smith (1961).

Psalm 19

1 John Stott, *Favourite Psalms: Growing Closer to God* (Mill Hill: Monarch Books, 1988), p. 18.
2 Ibid. pp. 18–21.
3 Michael Wilcock, *The Message of Psalms 1–72* (Nottingham: Inter-Varsity Press, 2001), p. 71.
4 Derek Kidner, *Psalms 1–72* (Downers Grove, IL: Inter-Varsity Press, 2008), p. 114.
5 Edward J. Young, *The Book of Isaiah* (Grand Rapids, MI: Eerdmans, 1965), Vol. 1, pp. 245–46.
6 See, for example, Acts 14:17, 17:22–28; Rom. 1:20, 10:18–20.
7 Joseph Addison, 'The spacious firmament on high' (1712).
8 Isaac Watts, 'The heavens declare Thy glory, Lord' (1719).
9 'The law' (in the Hebrew, torah) refers not just to God's law given to Moses, but the whole of Old Testament scripture.
10 I am grateful to Mike Cain, the senior pastor of Emmanuel Church, Bristol, for this, taken from his exposition of Psalm 19 on 28 April 2020. Accessed at emmanuelbristol.org.uk/category/mike-cain accessed on 29 May 2020.

11 Bishop Christopher Wordsworth (1872).

Psalm 20

1 John Richard Green, *History of the English People* (London: Macmillan, 1885), Vol. 1, p. 542.

2 See, for example, 1 Samuel 23:2, 30:8; 2 Samuel 5:19.

3 Derek Kidner, *Psalms 1–72* (Downers Grove, IL: Inter-Varsity Press, 2008), p. 119.

4 If you want to remind yourself of the details, it's the Jacob's ladder story in Genesis 28, specifically verses 13–15.

5 Quoted in *The Mail* on Sunday, 15 January 2017. Accessed online at dailymail.co.uk on 31 May 2020.

6 Gerald H. Wilson, *The NIV Application Commentary: Psalms Volume 1* (Grand Rapids, MI: Zondervan 2002), p. 390.

7 Edith G. Cherry, 'We rest on Thee, our shield and our defender' (1903).

Psalm 21

1 Dale Ralph Davis, *Slogging Along in the Paths of Righteousness* (Fearn, Ross-shire: Christian Focus, 2014), p. 141.

2 Quoted by James Montgomery Boice, *Psalms: An Expositional Commentary* (Grand Rapids, MI: Baker Books, 1994), Vol. 1, p. 185.

3 Isaac Watts, 'Come let us join our cheerful songs' (1707).

Psalm 22

1 John Stott, *Favourite Psalms: Growing Closer to God* (Mill Hill: Monarch Books, 1988), p. 23.

2 Ibid.

3 J.J. Stewart Perowne, *The Book of Psalms* (Grand Rapids, MI: Zondervan, 1976), p. 239.

4 J.C. Ryle, *Expository Thoughts on the Gospels: Mark* (Edinburgh: Banner of Truth Trust, 2012), p. 274.

5 John Stott, *Favourite Psalms*, p. 25.

6 J.J. Stewart Perowne, *The Book of Psalms*, p. 237.

7 Jonathan Evans, 'Hark! the voice of love and mercy' (1784).

Psalm 23

1 Robert Lowth, quoted in William S. Plumer, *Psalms* (1867 reprint, Edinburgh: Banner of Truth, 1975), p. 308.

2 Respectively Psalms 5:2, 7:11, 3:3, 18:2, 9:9.

3 Henry Blunt, *Posthumous Sermons* (London: Hatchard, 1845), Vol. 2, p. 157.

4 Ibid. pp. 159–60.

5 Matthew Henry, *Commentary on the Whole Bible* (Peabody, MA: Hendrickson, 2009), Vol. 3, p. 259.

6 Henry W. Baker, 'The King of Love My Shepherd Is' (1868).

Psalm 24

1 Charles Spurgeon, *The Treasury of David* (Peabody, MA: Hendrickson, 2016), Vol. 1, p. 375.

2 David Dickson, *A Commentary on the Psalms* (Edinburgh: Banner of Truth Trust, 1985), p. 126.

3 J.J. Stewart Perowne, *The Book of Psalms* (Grand Rapids, MI: Zondervan, 1976), p. 257.

4 See Ephesians 4:8–10; 1 Thessalonians 1:10; 1 Peter 3:22; Hebrews 1:4, 4:14, 9:24.

5 Charles Spurgeon, p. 378.

6 Ibid. p. 375.

7 Georg Weissel, 'Lift up your heads, you mighty gates' (1642).

Psalm 25

1 See, for example, Acts 9:2; 19:9, 23; 24:14, 22.

2 William Cowper, 'Jesus, where'er Thy people meet' (1769).

3 John H. Sammis, 'When we walk with the Lord' (1887).

4 Charles Bridges, *Proverbs* (Edinburgh: Banner of Truth, 1968), pp. 3–4.

5 Edwin P. Hood, 'O walk with Jesus' (1862).

Psalm 26

1   I am grateful to Christopher Ash for suggesting the theme of assurance in Psalm 26, from a sermon preached in St Andrew the Great, Cambridge, 10 November 2019. The sub-headings used in this chapter are adapted from his sermon, 'Being Sure for the Future.'

2   'The Letter of Athanasius, Archbishop of Alexandria to Marcellinus on the Interpretation of the Psalms' www.athanasius.com/psalms/aletterm.html. Accessed 27 June 2020.

3   Michael Wilcock, *The Message of Psalms 1–72* (Nottingham: Inter-Varsity Press, 2001), p. 95.

4   Alec Motyer, *Psalms By The Day* (Fearn, Ross-shire: Christian Focus, 2016), p. 72.

5   'How firm a foundation, ye saints of the Lord' (1787). Author unknown.

Psalm 27

1   E.C. Dawson (Editor), *The Last Journals of Bishop Hannington* (London: Seeley, 1888), p. 237.

2   Quoted, but not attributed, by John Stott, *Favourite Psalms: Growing Closer to God* (Mill Hill: Monarch Books, 2003), p. 32.

3   William Cowper, 'Hark! my soul, it is the Lord' (c. 1765).

4   Charles Wesley, 'Jesus, my strength, my hope' (1742).

Psalm 28

1   Dale Ralph Davis, I*n the Presence of My Enemies: Psalms 25–37* (Fearn, Ross-shire: Christian Focus, 2020), p. 66.

2   James Montgomery, 'Lord, teach us how to pray aright' (1818).

3   Quoting Deuteronomy 32:35.

4   Derek W.H. Thomas, *Acts* (Phillipsburg, NJ: P&R Publishing, 2011), p. 288.

5   R.A. Torrey, *The Power of Prayer* (Alachua, FL: Bridge-Logos, 2009), pp. 30–31.

6 Matthew Henry, *Commentary on the Whole Bible* (Peabody, MA: Hendrickson, 1991), Vol. 3, p. 274.

7 Augustus M. Toplady, 'A sovereign Protector I have' (1774) (© In this version Praise Trust).

Psalm 29

1 Harry Ironside, *Studies on Book One of the Psalms* (Neptune, NJ: Loizeaux, 1952), p. 171.

2 Robert Grant, 'O Worship the King' (1833).

3 Charles H. Spurgeon, *The Treasury of David* (Peabody, MA: Hendrickson, 2016), Vol. 1, Part 2, p. 32.

4 Gerald H. Wilson, *Psalms: The NIV Application Commentary* (Grand Rapids, MI: Zondervan, 2002), Vol. 1, pp. 511–12.

5 Robert Grant, 'O Worship the King' (1833).

Psalm 30

1 James Montgomery Boice, *Psalms: An Expositional Commentary* (Grand Rapids, MI: Baker Books, 1994), Vol. 1, p. 260.

2 Commentators vary as to their view on this. Gerald Wilson favours 'Temple' whilst Alec Motyer prefers 'House'. Most commentators merely present both — or other — options.

3 See Alec Motyer, *Treasures of the King: Psalms from the Life of David* (Nottingham: Inter-Varsity Press, 2007), p. 99.

4 Derek Kidner, *Psalms 1–72* (Downers Grove, IL: Inter-Varsity Press, 2008), p. 146.

5 Alec Motyer, *Treasures of the King*, p. 102.

6 J.J. Stewart Perowne, *The Book of Psalms* (Grand Rapids, MI: Zondervan, 1976), p. 280. To see its use in that context, see Jeremiah 14:8.

7 Ibid.

8 Ibid.

9 John S.B. Monsell, 'O worship the Lord in the beauty of holiness' (1863).

Psalm 31

1 Franz Delitzsch, *Commentary on the Old Testament* (Peabody, MA: Hendrickson, 2006, reprint), Vol. 5, p. 246.
2 William F. Lloyd (1835).
3 Delitzsch, *Commentary on the Old Testament*, p. 250.

Psalm 32

1 John Stott, *Favourite Psalms: Growing Closer to God* (Mill Hill: Monarch Books, 2003), p. 38.
2 Charles H. Spurgeon, *The Treasury of David* (Peabody, MA: Hendrickson, 2016), Vol. 1, Part 2, p. 82.
3 This illustration is used by John Phillips, *Exploring Psalms: An Expository Commentary* (Grand Rapids, MI: Kregel, 1988), Vol. 1, p. 244.
4 Timothy Dudley-Smith, 'Happy are those, beyond all measure blessed' © 2008 Author/Oxford University Press.

Psalm 33

1 Quoted in John Risbridger, *The Message of Worship* (Nottingham: Inter-Varsity Press, 2015), p. 22.
2 Robert G. Rayburn, *O Come, Let Us Worship: Corporate Worship in the Evangelical Church* (Eugene, OR: Wipf & Stock, 2010), p. 11.
3 Paul S. Jones, *What is Worship Music?* (Phillipsburg, NJ: P&R Publishing, 2010), pp. 8, 19, 27.
4 Franz Delitzsch, *Commentary on the Psalms* (Peabody, MA: Hendrickson, 2006), p. 258.
5 James Montgomery (1819).
6 Delitzsch, p. 259.
7 Reginald Heber, 'Brightest and best of the sons of the morning' (1811).

Psalm 34

1 Alec Motyer, *Treasures of the King: Psalms from the Life of David* (Nottingham: Inter-Varsity Press, 2007), p. 32.

2   Derek Kidner, *Psalms 1–72* (Downers Grove, IL: Inter-Varsity Press, 2008), p. 156.

3   Verses 1, 3, 4, 7, 8 and 9, which is why the hymn in its current format seems to come to something of an abrupt end.

4   Nahum Tate and Nicholas Brady, 'Through all the changing scenes of life', in *A New Version of the Psalms of David* (1754). Accessed at www.hymnary.org, 20 July 2020.

5   Ibid.

6   Derek Kidner, p. 158.

7   In the following chapter, he quotes vv. 12–16 of Psalm 34 which appear as 1 Peter 3:10–12.

8   A.M. Stibbs, *1 Peter* (Leicester: Inter-Varsity Press, 1959), p. 97.

Psalm 35

1   William Walsham How, 'It is a thing most wonderful' (1872).

2   Allan Harman, *Psalms 1–72* (Fearn, Ross-shire: Christian Focus, 2011), p. 84.

3   Derek Kidner, *Psalms 1–72* (Downers Grove, IL: Inter-Varsity Press, 2008), p. 160.

4   Alec Motyer, *Psalms by the Day* (Fearn, Ross-shire: Christian Focus, 2016), p. 94.

5   Thomas B. Pollock, 'We have not known Thee as we ought' (1889).

Psalm 36

1   To read of God's covenant with King David, see 2 Samuel 7. In the same way, Jesus spoke of the new covenant (see Mark 14:24) a theme taken up in the epistles (see, for example, Hebrews 8:6–13).

2   Arthur W. Pink, *The Attributes of God* (Grand Rapids, MI: Baker, 1975), p. 67.

3   Derek Kidner, *Psalms 1–72* (Downers Grove, IL: Inter-Varsity Press, 2008), p. 165.

4 Ibid.

5 Gerald H. Wilson, *Psalms: The NIV Application Commentary* (Grand Rapids, MI: Zondervan, 2002), Vol. 1, p. 593.

6 Horatius Bonar, 'O love of God, how strong and true' (1861). In this version, Trinity Hymnal (1961).

Psalm 37

1 See Psalm 25.

2 James Montgomery Boice, *Psalms: An Expositional Commentary* (Grand Rapids, MI: Baker, 1994), Vol. 1, p. 326.

3 Franz Delitzsch, *Commentary on the Old Testament: Psalms* (Peabody, MA: Hendrickson, 2006), p. 283.

4 Ibid.

5 Rowland Hill, 'Cast your burden on the Lord' (1783).

Psalm 38

1 The others are Psalms 6, 32, 51, 102, 130 and 143.

2 *Book of Common Prayer* (1662), Service of Commination.

3 Charles Spurgeon, *The Treasury of David* (Peabody, MA: Hendrickson, 2016), Vol. 1, Part 2, p. 202.

4 John R. W. Stott, *The Cross of Christ* (Nottingham: Inter-Varsity Press, 1989), p. 116.

5 W.S. Plumer, *Psalms: A Critical and Expository Commentary* (Edinburgh: Banner of Truth, 1975) p. 464.

6 Charles Wesley (1742).

7 Quoted in Plumer, *Psalms*, p. 466.

8 Michael Saward, 'In awe and wonder, Lord our God' (© Author/ Jubilate Hymns)

Psalm 39

1 Alec Motyer, *Psalms by the Day* (Fearn, Ross-shire: Christian Focus, 2016), p. 104.

2 Franz Delitzsch, *Commentary on the Old Testament: Psalms* (Peabody, MA: Hendrickson, 2006), p. 295.

3   Christopher Ash, *Job: The Wisdom of the Cross* (Wheaton, IL: Crossway, 2014), pp. 130–131.
4   James Montgomery Boice, *Psalms: An Expositional Commentary* (Grand Rapids, MI: Baker, 1994), Vol. 1, p. 343.
5   Ibid.
6   William Shakespeare, *Macbeth*, Act V, Scene 5.
7   Henry Francis Lyte, 'Jesus, I my cross have taken' (1825).

Psalm 40

1   James Boice, *Psalms: An Expositional Commentary* (Grand Rapids, MI: Baker, 1994), Vol. 1, pp. 348–349.
2   Also see Psalm 51:16–17; Isaiah 1:10–17; Jeremiah 7:21–26; Micah 6:6–8.
3   Richard D. Phillips, *Hebrews* (Phillipsburg, NJ: P & R Publishing, 2006), p 339.
4   Isaac Watts (1709), in *Hymns for Today's Church* (1982).

Psalm 41

1   Derek Kidner, *Psalms 1–72* (Downers Grove, IL: Inter-Varsity Press, 2008), p. 179.
2   Ibid.
3   Knox Chamblin, *Matthew* (Fearn, Ross-shire: Christian Focus, 2010), Vol. 2, p. 1259.
4   See Matthew 27:5 –'And throwing down the pieces of silver into the temple, [Judas] departed, and he went and hanged himself.'
5   John Newton, 'Glorious things of Thee are spoken' (1779).